Cambridge First Certificate
Examination Practice 2

# Cambridge First Certificate

# Examination Practice 2

*University of Cambridge
Local Examinations Syndicate*

**Cambridge University Press**
Cambridge
New York   Port Chester
Melbourne   Sydney

Published by the Press Syndicate of the University of Cambridge
The Pitt Building, Trumpington Street, Cambridge CB2 1RP
40 West 20th Street, New York, NY 10011, USA
10 Stamford Road, Oakleigh, Melbourne 3166, Australia

© Cambridge University Press 1986

First published 1986
Sixth printing 1990

Printed in Great Britain
at The Bath Press, Avon

ISBN 0 521 33902 2  Student's Book
ISBN 0 521 33903 0  Teacher's Book
ISBN 0 521 32589 7  Set of 2 cassettes

**Copyright**
The law allows a reader to make a single copy of part of a book
for purposes of private study. It does not allow the copying of
entire books or the making of multiple copies of extracts. Written
permission for any such copying must always be obtained from the
publisher in advance.

KV

# Contents

**To the student**  1

**Practice Test 1**  2

**Practice Test 2**  21

**Practice Test 3**  40

**Practice Test 4**  60

**Practice Test 5**  78

**Interview Exercises**  98

**Acknowledgements**  115

**Answer Sheets**  116

# To the student

This book is for candidates preparing for the University of Cambridge First Certificate in English examination and provides practice in all the written and oral papers. It contains 5 complete tests, based on the First Certificate examinations set in 1984 and 1985, and incorporates the modifications made to Paper 5 (the Interview) in December 1985. The examination consists of 5 papers, as follows:

Paper 1 Reading Comprehension (1 hour)
  Section A consists of 25 multiple-choice items in the form of a sentence with a blank to be filled by 1 of 4 words or phrases.
  Section B consists of 15 multiple-choice items based on 3 or more reading passages of different types.

Paper 2 Composition (1½ hours)
  There are 5 topics from which you choose 2. Each composition must be between 120 and 180 words in length. (In these practice tests the questions based on optional reading are set on the kind of books that are prescribed each year. These are *not* the actual books prescribed for any particular year: they are just given as examples.)

Paper 3 Use of English (2 hours)
  There are exercises of various kinds which test your control of English usage and grammatical structure and a directed writing exercise where you extract information from a text and present it in a coherent form.

Paper 4 Listening Comprehension (20 to 30 minutes)
  You answer a variety of questions on recorded passages (normally 3) from English broadcasts, interviews, announcements, phone messages and conversations. Each passage is heard twice.

Paper 5 Interview (15 to 20 minutes)
  You take part in a conversation based on a photograph, passage and other material from authentic sources linked by theme, either with a group of other candidates or with the examiner alone. The exercises in these tests include some of the type set in the examination on optional reading.

# Practice Test 1

## PAPER 1   READING COMPREHENSION   (1 hour)

*Answer all questions. Indicate your choice of answer in every case* **on the separate answer sheet** *already given out, which should show your name and examination index number. Follow carefully the instructions about how to record your answers. Give* **one answer only** *to each question. Marks will not be deducted for wrong answers: your total score on this test will be the number of correct answers you give.*

### SECTION A

*In this section you must choose the word or phrase which best completes each sentence.* **On your answer sheet** *indicate the letter A, B, C, or D against the number of each item 1 to 25 for the word or phrase you choose.*

1  It's a good idea to see your doctor regularly for ............... .
   A  a revision    B  a control    C  an investigation    D  a check-up

2  I lost too much money betting at the races last time, so you won't ............... me to go again.
   A  convince    B  impress    C  persuade    D  urge

3  Last year the potato harvest was very disappointing, but this year it looks as though we shall have a better ............... .
   A  product    B  outcome    C  amount    D  crop

4  The shop assistant was ............... helpful, but she felt he could have given her more advice.
   A  entirely    B  exactly    C  quite    D  totally

5  When the starter gave the ............... all the competitors in the race began to run round the track.
   A  signal    B  warning    C  shot    D  show

6  It's an awful ............... your wife couldn't come. I was looking forward to meeting her.
   A  harm    B  sorrow    C  shame    D  shock

7  ............... from Bill, all the students said they would go.
   A  Except    B  Only    C  Apart    D  Separate

[2]

Practice Test 1

8  The new manager explained to the staff that she hoped to ............... new procedures to save time and money.
   A manufacture   B establish   C control   D restore

9  There is a fault at our television station. Please do not ............... your set.
   A change   B adjust   C repair   D switch

10 He was an ............... writer because he persuaded many people to see the truth of his ideas.
   A ordinary   B influential   C unlimited   D accurate

11 The meal was excellent; the pears were particularly ................
   A flavoured   B delicious   C tasteful   D desirable

12 Workers who do not obey the safety regulations will be ............... immediately.
   A refused   B rejected   C disapproved   D dismissed

13 He was in ............... of a large number of men.
   A management   B leadership   C charge   D direction

14 ............... goes the bus; now we will have to walk!
   A On time   B At once   C There   D Early

15 When he retired from his job the directors ............... him with a clock.
   A offered   B pleased   C satisfied   D presented

16 He had to leave his family ............... when he went abroad to work.
   A at a loss   B behind   C out   D at all costs

17 I am very ............... in the information you have given me.
   A concerned   B surprised   C interesting   D interested

18 When I went to talk to the manager, he told me he could only ............... me a few minutes.
   A provide   B spare   C hear   D let

19 I saw a thief take Norman's wallet so I ran ............... him, but I didn't catch him.
   A into   B after   C over   D near

20 If it's raining tomorrow, we shall have to ............... the match till Sunday.
   A put off   B cancel   C play   D put away

21 It is usually better not to ............... things, in case they are not returned.
   A lend   B offer   C borrow   D lose

[3]

Practice Test 1

22  He opened the letter without .............. to read the address on the envelope.
    A worrying    B caring    C fearing    D bothering

23  There was a big hole in the road which .............. the traffic.
    A held up    B kept down    C stood back    D sent back

24  The boy fell into the river and was .............. along by the fast current.
    A caught    B swept    C thrown    D swung

25  The old sailing boat was .............. without trace during the fierce storm.
    A lost    B crashed    C disappeared    D vanished

## SECTION B

*In this section you will find after each of the passages a number of questions or unfinished statements about the passage, each with four suggested answers or ways of finishing. You must choose the one which you think fits best.* **On your answer sheet, indicate the letter A, B, C or D against the number of each item 26–40 for the answer you choose. Give one answer only to each question. Read each passage right through before choosing your answers.**

FIRST PASSAGE

Frances Wingate had not been to Tockley for many years – she could not remember how many. Her grandfather had died when she was fourteen. Her grandmother had died ten years later, but she had been out of the country at the time and had not gone to the funeral. In fact, after her grandfather's death she had hardly visited Tockley at all, she now remembered guiltily: the place had begun to depress her. She could no longer stand the slow pace, the quietness, the emptiness, the very things that had charmed her as a small child, and her grandmother had turned odd and difficult to live with, even more bad-tempered than she had been when younger, even more given to sudden bursts of anger and long silences.

She thought of it, then as now, as 'going to Tockley', but the house wasn't really in Tockley: it was about six miles out, a distance that had then seemed enormous, as it had to be travelled by bus. The town was a medium-sized ordinary town, with much light industry; it was easy enough to get to, but it was the kind of place one goes through, rather than stops at. Frances had booked a room at the Railway Hotel, because it was next to the station, and because her guide-book said it was well run and that the food was quite good. She looked out of the window of the train and wondered what she remembered of the town. Little, she thought. It hadn't meant much to her grandparents: they went there once a fortnight to shop, depending otherwise on the shop in the nearest village and on what they produced in their

[4]

Practice Test 1

own garden. There was a famous church, rising out of the flat plain, which could be seen for miles: her guide-book described it with some excitement, but she didn't remember that she had ever been in it. She remembered the wool shop, the shoe shop, the grocer's a little. It had probably all changed by now.

The cottage, too, had probably changed. She remembered it in great detail. It had been the one fixed point in her childhood; for her parents had always been moving from one house to another as her father had been promoted from one academic post to the next; five years here, three years there, had been the pattern. Granny Ollerenshaw, in the cottage, had been immovable, unchanged and unchanging. They called it Eel Cottage: over the doorway there was a square sign which announced EEL 1779. For years Frances had though that this meant the fish which lived in muddy ditches; only later, looking more closely, did she realise that the mysterious word must have been the builder's or owner's initials. The cottage was a basic cottage, the kind that small children draw: low, a door in the middle, two windows downstairs, two windows upstairs. It was built of red brick, the brick of the district, with a red-tiled steep roof.

26  Why didn't Frances remember very much about Tockley?
    A  There was nothing special in the town.
    B  She had only been there once or twice.
    C  She had been abroad for a long time.
    D  The town had changed a great deal since her childhood.

27  Where was Frances' grandparents' house?
    A  on the edge of Tockley
    B  near the shops in Tockley
    C  in a village on a bus route from Tockley
    D  in the countryside some miles from Tockley

28  Why was Frances' grandparents' house called "Eel Cottage"?
    A  Eels used to be common in the area.
    B  Someone's initials had spelt the word 'Eel'.
    C  The first owner had been called Mr Eel.
    D  No-one knew why.

29  Why did Frances stop visiting the cottage regularly?
    A  She had been leading a very busy life.
    B  She had quarrelled with her grandmother.
    C  She had come to dislike the place.
    D  She had lost touch with her family.

30  Why had her grandparents' house meant a lot to Frances as a child?
    A  She had been brought up happily there.
    B  The shape and colour of the house had attracted her.
    C  She had felt things would never change there.
    D  She had been lonely as a child.

[5]

Practice Test 1

SECOND PASSAGE

Trees should only be pruned when there is a good and clear reason for doing so and, fortunately, the number of such reasons is small. Pruning involves the cutting away of overgrown and unwanted branches, and the inexperienced gardener can be encouraged by the thought that more damage results from doing it unnecessarily than from leaving the tree to grow in its own way.

First, pruning may be done to make sure that trees have a desired shape or size. The object may be to get a tree of the right height, and at the same time to help the growth of small side branches which will thicken its appearance or give it a special shape. Secondly, pruning may be done to make the tree healthier. You may cut out diseased or dead wood, or branches that are rubbing against each other and thus causing wounds. The health of a tree may be encouraged by removing branches that are blocking up the centre and so preventing the free movement of air.

One result of pruning is that an open wound is left on the tree and this provides an easy entry for disease, but it is a wound that will heal. Often there is a race between the healing and the disease as to whether the tree will live or die, so that there is a period when the tree is at risk. It should be the aim of every gardener to reduce that risk of death as far as possible. It is essential to make the area which has been pruned smooth and clean, for healing will be slowed down by roughness. You should allow the cut surface to dry for a few hours and then paint it with one of the substances available from garden shops produced especially for this purpose. Pruning is usually done in winter, for then you can see the shape of the tree clearly without interference from the leaves and it is, too, very unlikely that the cuts you make will bleed. If this does happen, it is, of course, impossible to paint them properly.

31  Pruning should be done to
    A  make the tree grow taller.
    B  improve the shape of the tree.
    C  get rid of the small branches.
    D  make the small branches thicker.

32  Trees become unhealthy if the gardener
    A  allows too many branches to grow in the middle.
    B  does not protect them from the wind.
    C  forces them to grow too quickly.
    D  damages some of the small side branches.

33  Why is a special substance painted on the tree?
    A  to make a wound smooth
    B  to prevent disease entering a wound
    C  to cover a rough surface
    D  to help a wound to dry

[6]

34 A good gardener prunes a tree
    A  at intervals throughout the year.
    B  as quickly as possible.
    C  occasionally when necessary.
    D  regularly every Winter.

35 What was the author's purpose when writing this passage?
    A  to give practical instructions for pruning a tree
    B  to give a general description of pruning
    C  to explain how trees develop diseases
    D  to discuss different methods of pruning

[7]

Practice Test 1

THIRD PASSAGE

You go to a book stall to choose some books for a long train journey. You pick some up and read what it says about them on the back covers.
Read the following extracts from the book descriptions and then answer the questions.

## Book A

...The Roman Emperor Claudius writes the inside story of his public life. Men classed him as a pitiful fool. But the actions he decribes are far from foolish. Reluctantly crowned Emperor, he appears as a man whose errors came from good nature and innocence. It is the common people and the common soldiers who help him to repair the damage done by the Emperor Caligula by conquering Britain, and who stand by him in his final hard judgement on his unfaithful wife, Messalina.

This is one of the finest historical reconstructions published this century...

## Book B

...A fortune-teller once told Mary (as the author calls herself in this book): "You are going to be loved by people you've never seen and never will see".
That statement came true when she published her delightful and exact record of country life at the end of the last century – a record in which she describes the fast-dissolving England of farm-worker and country tradesman and colours her picture with the cheerful courage and the rare pleasures that marked a self-sufficient world of work and poverty...

## Book C

..."Leave it to my man, Johnson," Cecil used to say, whether the problem was the colour of a shirt, the shape of a hat, the style of a coat. What did it matter if Johnson tended to take charge of his life and that without his approval his employer could not even grow a moustache? Was he not always there for him to lean on in moments of difficulty?
And such moments were frequent in the leisured life of Cecil and his friends in the London of the first motor buses.

Practice Test 1

*Book D*

> ...The novel is the story of a man for whom both real life and university research have lost their meaning. Separated from his over-emotional wife, Gerald Middleton is painfully aware that the centre of his life is empty. But the world is reaching out for him again...
>
> Gerald is the only person still alive who was present when Bishop Eorpwald's grave was opened and the strange wooden figure found which has offended, puzzled and fascinated students of early English history for years. But he also keeps another even worse secret...

36. Which book will probably be light and humourous?
    A. Book A
    B. Book B
    C. Book C
    D. Book D

37. Which book seems to be set in the present day?
    A. Book A
    B. Book B
    C. Book C
    D. Book D

38. From the information given here, the Emperor Claudius appears to have been
    A. a foolish ruler.
    B. an ambitious man.
    C. a successful general.
    D. a forgiving husband.

39. Gerald Middleton appears to be a
    A. professor of history.
    B. private detective.
    C. writer of crime stories.
    D. university student.

40. What was the relationship between Johnson and Cecil?
    A. Johnson ordered Cecil to do things.
    B. Johnson never questioned orders.
    C. Cecil depended on Johnson.
    D. Cecil paid Johnson well.

[9]

*Practice Test 1*

## PAPER 2  COMPOSITION  (1½ hours)

*Write **two only** of the following composition exercises. Your answers must follow exactly the instructions given and must be of between 120 and 180 words each.*

1  You came to London a month ago to study English. Write a letter to your parents, telling them about the course you are taking and some of the difficulties you have encountered.

2  The students in your college think the food and service in the canteen are very poor. The Principal of the college has agreed to listen to your complaints and to discuss suggestions for improvement. Write what you would say to him.

3  You were visiting some friends in their flat late one evening when you heard someone shout 'Fire'! Describe what happened next.

4  Unemployment, especially among young people, is a serious problem in many countries today. What can be done about it? Do you think traditional ideas about work should be changed?

5  Based on your reading of any one of these books, write on *one* of the following.

   JANE AUSTEN: *Sense and Sensibility*
   Who is Colonel Brandon, and what part does he play in the novel?

   G. B. SHAW: *Arms and the Man*
   When Bluntschli leaves after hiding in Raina's bedroom, she gives him her father's old coat to disguise him. Explain what happens to the coat after that.

   GRAHAM GREENE: *The Third Man*
   There are two funerals in this story and both are for Harry Lime. Explain how this came about.

[10]

PAPER 3  USE OF ENGLISH  (2 hours)

1  Fill each of the numbered blanks in the following passage. Use only **one** word in each space.

Carter was usually able to catch the 6.35 train from Euston. This brought ..........(1) to the town where he lived at 7.12. His bicycle waited ..........(2) him at the station – the ticket-collector always looked ..........(3) it for him. Then he ..........(4) home, changing his route from day to day. He crossed the canal ..........(5), turned ..........(6) the church and up the hill to his small, semi-detached house ..........(7) Queens Road. He had ..........(8) it on his return to England and although he ..........(9) have afforded a much bigger house, he had no wish to draw attention to himself ..........(10) the source of his income. He always arrived home at 7.30, unless he had ..........(11) Sarah, his wife, to say that he would be ..........(12) late. There was just time ..........(13) say goodnight to his baby son and have a whisky or two before dinner at 8.00.

When he ..........(14) the door of his house he saw that the hall was empty, and there was no sound from the kitchen. He noticed at ..........(15) that the whisky bottle was not standing ready on the small table in the living-room. The habit of years had ..........(16) broken and Carter felt anxious. He called, 'Sarah!' but there was ..........(17) reply. He had always, ..........(18) they returned ..........(19) England, known that this moment ..........(20) come, and he tried not to panic.

[11]

*Practice Test 1*

2  Finish each of the following sentences in such a way that it means exactly the same as the sentence printed before it.

EXAMPLE: I haven't enjoyed myself so much for years.

ANSWER: It's years *since I enjoyed myself so much.*

a) 'Why don't you put a better lock on the door, Barry?' said John.
   John suggested Barry putting a better lock on the door.

b) Although both his legs were broken in the crash, he managed to get out of the car before it exploded.
   Despite his legs broken in the crash, he managed to get broken legs out of the car before it exploded.

c) I haven't eaten this kind of food before.
   This is the first time I have eaten this kind of food.

d) After fighting the fire for twelve hours the firemen succeeded in putting it out.
   The firemen managed to succeed in putting the fire out after fighting the fire for twelve hours.

e) The architect has drawn plans for an extension to the house.
   Plans have been drawn for an extension to the house by the architect.

f) In Stratford-on-Avon we saw Shakespeare's birthplace.
   We saw the house where Shakespeare was born in Stratford.

g) It isn't necessary for you to finish by Saturday.
   You have to finish it by Saturday.

h) 'How many survivors are there?' asked the journalist.
   The journalist wanted to know how many survivors there were.

i) It was such rotten meat that it had to be thrown away.
   The meat was so rotten that it had to be thrown away.

j) It is essential that Professor Van Helsing is met at the airport.
   Professor Van Helsing has to be met at the airport.

[12]

3  Complete the following sentences with **one** appropriate word connected with the subject of **money**.

> EXAMPLE: His *salary* is paid into his bank account every month.

a) You can't pay by cheque or credit card. They only accept ...cash... ✓

b) What is the ............... rate of the pound today? exchange ✓

c) During the sale the shop will give a 20% ...discount... on all purchases over £100. ✓

d) Because of losing his job he can hardly find the money to re-pay his bank ...credit... (loan)

e) If you invest £100,000 in our bank for one year, we will pay you 10% ...interest... ✓

4  Complete the following sentences with an expression formed from **turn**.

> EXAMPLE: They expected two hundred people to come to the meeting but only seventy turned *up*. ✓

a) The radio is too loud. Turn it ...down...

b) The concert was so popular that people who had not bought tickets in advance were turned ...back... at the door. (away) ✗

c) The large vase in which he had kept his umbrella for many years turned ...in... (out) to be a valuable piece of Chinese pottery. ✗

d) She was standing at the end of the pier looking out to sea and I waited for her to turn ...over... (round) so that I could see her face. ✗

e) Without any warning the dog, which had been lying quietly on the grass, turned ...on... the postman and bit him. ✓

[13]

Practice Test 1

5  Make all the changes and additions necessary to produce, from the following sets of words and phrases, sentences which together make a complete letter. Note carefully from the example what kind of alterations need to be made. Write each sentence in the space provided.

EXAMPLE: I / wonder / why you / not / reply / last letter.

ANSWER: I was wondering why you had not replied to my last letter.

Dear Sir,

I / very surprised / letter / I receive / you this morning.

a) I was very surprised by the letter I have received from you this morning.

In it / say / I not pay / book / send / one month ago.

b) In it you said that I had not payed for the book you sent to me one month ago.

You say / I / send / money immediately.

c) You said that I have to should send the money immediately.

In fact / I return / book / you / same day / receive.

d) In fact I returned the book to you the same day I receive it.

I not return / because / not want.

e) I did not return it because I did not want it.

But because / book / be / poor condition / several torn pages.

f) But because the book was in poor condition with several torn pages.

I send / letter / that time / ask you / send / perfect copy / same book.

g) I sent a letter at that time asking you to send me a perfect copy of the same book.

I hope / you do that and / not have / write / you again / this matter.

h) I hope you are going to do that and that I won't have to write you again about this matter.

Yours faithfully,
Samuel Johnson

[14]

6  Read the following passages about some proposed property developments in the town of Melchester, and look also at the instructions on page 16.

**From 'An Architectural Guide to Britain':**

**MELCHESTER** (pop. 65,000)
The town is attractively situated on the River Ouse and dates from the ninth century. Despite its great age the town has few buildings of interest. In the last ten years there has been a lot of 'development' – new Town Hall, library, bus station, railway station. Perhaps the only building in the town which the visitor should make a point of seeing is the Old Grammar School. Built in the early seventeenth century by a rich local merchant, Sir William Waller, it is one of the oldest school buildings in England and is a perfect example of the style of that period. There is a magnificent exterior and inside some fine ceilings and panelled walls.

**From the 'Melchester Times':**

**OLD SCHOOL TO MOVE TO NEW SITE**

MR DAVID WALLER, Chairman of the Governors of the Old Grammar School has announced that a new school will be built on the outskirts of Melchester. To raise money for this the Old Grammar School is to be sold. 'The school is on a prime site in the centre of town. It may look beautiful from the outside but inside it is in a terrible state: It is dark and gloomy and there is little fresh air or light. It is more suitable for rabbits than schoolboys. It is costing us too much to keep on repairing it'. He added that Mega Properties had made a 'substantial offer' for the site.

---

MEMO:  URGENT

FROM:  Lord Grabbit, Chairman of Mega Properties

TO:  Peter Smooth, Publicity Officer, Mega Properties

Apparently certain people in Melchester are opposed to our plans to demolish the Old Grammar School and build a new shopping centre on the site and are calling for the Minister of the Environment to hold an inquiry. Please prepare some publicity material to be sent to local newspapers and influential local people in the town. Point out that both the construction of the centre and the shops themselves will provide jobs for the people of Melchester where there is a lot of unemployment. Explain that the interior of the school is in such a poor state that it cannot be used for any purpose. The site is too important to have an empty or underused building on it and more people will come to shop in the shopping centre than come to look at the school.

---

**To the editor of the 'Melchester Times':**

Dear Sir,
We are very disturbed by reports that the Old Grammar School is to be demolished by Mega Properties. Our town has already lost many of its historic old buildings which have been replaced by boring examples of modern architecture (several of them built by Mega Properties). The Old Grammar School is a building of great historical and architectural significance – to destroy it would be an act of vandalism. We are in favour of keeping the building and renovating the interior which could be used for offices, evening classes, exhibitions, a meeting place for local clubs and societies and many other purposes.
Yours faithfully,
JOHN KEEP,
Chairman,
Melchester Heritage Society

[15]

*Practice Test 1*

> To the editor of the 'Melchester Times':
>
> Dear Sir,
> I have been following with great interest the debate in your columns between those who wish to keep the Old Grammar School and those who wish to see a new shopping centre on the site. May I suggest a compromise? Most people seem to agree that it is the exterior of the building which is beautiful. Why not keep the exterior frontage and build a shopping centre behind it, demolishing only the interior of the school? That way we could have the shopping centre and the best part of the school. As an architect, I know that this can be done.
> Yours faithfully,
> JOHN NASH

> MEMO:
>
> FROM: Lord Grabbit
>
> TO: Peter Smooth
>
> Support seems to be growing for the idea of keeping the exterior of the Old Grammar School. Attack this idea vigorously! It will be far cheaper and more convenient for us to demolish the entire school and start building on an empty site.

There are three proposals concerning the future of the Old Grammar School at Melchester. Describe each one in one sentence.

1 ................................................................................................................................
................................................................................................................................

2 ................................................................................................................................
................................................................................................................................

3 ................................................................................................................................
................................................................................................................................

Which do you think is the best proposal? Complete the following paragraph in not more than 100 words, giving reasons for the one you have chosen and taking into account its advantages and disadvantages.

I think the best proposal is to ................................................................................
................................................................................................................................
................................................................................................................................
................................................................................................................................
................................................................................................................................

[16]

Practice Test 1

# PAPER 4  LISTENING COMPREHENSION
(about 30 minutes)

### FIRST PART

*In the table below there are three people and eight statements about them. Decide which statements apply to each person and tick (✓) the appropriate boxes.*

|   |   | the woman | the man | the woman's friend at university |
|---|---|---|---|---|
| 1 | likes loud music at night | | | |
| 2 | likes working early in the morning | | | |
| 3 | likes listening to classical music | | | |
| 4 | likes to set a time limit | | | |
| 5 | likes to finish a specific topic in a day | | | |
| 6 | needs a lot of coffee when working | | | |
| 7 | sleeps during the afternoon | | | |
| 8 | likes to listen to loud music on the radio | | | |

[17]

*Practice Test 1*

## SECOND PART

For questions 9–20 tick (√) whether the statements are true or false.

|   |   | True | False |
|---|---|---|---|
| 9 | 'Tell All' is a 'phone-in' programme. | | |
| 10 | There were lots of letters about 'Weather Tomorrow'. | | |
| 11 | Mr J. Jones disagreed with Professor Strong's theory. | | |
| 12 | Mrs Marsh would like daily weather forecasts improved. | | |
| 13 | Changeable weather is preferred by a Scottish listener. | | |
| 14 | Food is a popular topic amongst listeners. | | |
| 15 | On Mondays there's a cookery series for men. | | |
| 16 | The Producer of 'Men in the Kitchen' is a woman. | | |
| 17 | Listeners will eventually be doing more difficult cookery. | | |
| 18 | The student has supplied her address. | | |
| 19 | Libraries will definitely charge 20 pence per book. | | |
| 20 | Spectacles and false teeth are free. | | |

[18]

## THIRD PART

Fill in the gaps 21–25 on the programme board shown below.

```
                          PROGRAMMES BEGINNING
                          Weekdays      Sundays         Prices

ABC 1 'The Captain's Lady'   1.00        (21) ...............
      (15 Cert.)             4.05         6.40           £2.10
                             7.10

ABC 2 'Starfighters'         1.10         3.30           £2.10
      (U Cert.)              4.20         6.30      children under 16
                             7.40                   (22) £ ...............

ABC 3 (23) ...............  ,(24) ............... 4.20
      (15 Cert.)             4.45         7.10           £2.10
                             7.30

REDUCED RATES FOR OVER-SIXTIES FOR AFTERNOON PERFORMANCES.
LATE SHOW ON (25) ............... : 'THE CAPTAIN'S LADY'
DOORS OPEN 10.45 P.M.
```

## FOURTH PART

For questions 26–30 tick (✓) whether you think the statements are true or false.

|   | True | False |
|---|------|-------|
| 26 You can hear the final instalment again next Friday morning. | | |
| 27 The next programme on Radio 4 is called 'Helston in Cornwall'. | | |
| 28 You can hear the football commentary at 9 o'clock. | | |
| 29 The programme 'Would you credit it?' is on Radio 3 at 10 o'clock. | | |
| 30 If you want to listen to the 'London Pop Spectacular', turn over to Radio 1. | | |

*Practice Test 1*

# PAPER 5   INTERVIEW   (about 15 minutes)

You will be asked to take part in a conversation with a group of other students or with your teacher. The conversation will be based on one particular topic area or theme, for example holidays, work, food.

Of course each interview will be different for each student or group of students, but a *typical* interview is described below.

* At the start of the interview you will be asked to talk about one of the photographs among the Interview Exercises at the back of the book.

* You will then be asked to discuss one of the passages at the back of the book. Your teacher may ask you to talk about its content, where you think it comes from, who the author or speaker is, whether you agree or disagree with it, and so on. You will *not* be asked to read the passage aloud, but you may quote parts of it to make your point.

* You may then be asked to discuss for example an advertisement, a leaflet, extract from a newspaper etc. Your teacher will tell you which of the Interview Exercises to look at.

* You may also be asked to take part in an activity with a group of other students or your teacher. Your teacher will tell you which section among the Interview Exercises you should look at.

# Practice Test 2

## PAPER 1    READING COMPREHENSION    (1 hour)

*Answer all questions. Indicate your choice of answer in every case* **on the separate answer sheet** *already given out, which should show your name and examination index number. Follow carefully the instructions about how to record your answers. Give* **one answer only** *to each question. Marks will not be deducted for wrong answers: your total score on this test will be the number of correct answers you give.*

### SECTION A

*In this section you must choose the word or phrase which best completes each sentence.* **On your answer sheet** *indicate the letter, A, B, C or D, against the number of each item 1 to 25 for the word or phrase you choose.*

1   You can learn as much theory as you like, but you only master a skill by .................. it a lot.
    A  practising    B  training    C  exercising    D  doing

2   Some people think it is .................. to use long and little-known words.
    A  clever    B  intentional    C  skilled    D  sensitive

3   The Chairman was so angry with the committee that he decided to .................. from it.
    A  cancel    B  postpone    C  resign    D  prevent

4   The explorers walked all the way along the river from its mouth to its ...................
    A  cause    B  well    C  source    D  outlet

5   He was afraid of losing his suitcase so he tied a .................. on it on which he had written his name and address.
    A  badge    B  mark    C  label    D  notice

6   He enjoyed the dessert so much that he accepted a second .................. when it was offered.
    A  load    B  pile    C  helping    D  sharing

[21]

*Practice Test 2*

7   He soon received promotion, for his superiors realised that he was a man of considerable .................. .
    A  ability      B  possibility     C  future      D  opportunity

8   Is there a bank where I can .................. these pounds for dollars?
    A  exchange    B  turn    C  alter    D  arrange

9   To our .................., Geoffrey's illness proved not to be as serious as we had feared.
    A  anxiety    B  eyes    C  relief    D  judgement

10  The author had qualified as a doctor but later gave up the .................. of medicine for full-time writing.
    A  practice    B  treatment    C  procedure    D  prescription

11  Don't touch the cat, he may .................. you.
    A  kick    B  tear    C  scream    D  scratch

12  Buy the new .................. of soap now on sale: it is softer than all others!
    A  model    B  brand    C  mark    D  manufacture

13  The chief of police said that he saw no .................. between the six murders.
    A  joint    B  connection    C  communication    D  join

14  The safety committee's report recommended that all medicines should be kept out of the .................. of children.
    A  hold    B  hand    C  reach    D  grasp

15  In the jar there was a .................. which looked like jam.
    A  substance    B  material    C  solid    D  powder

16  He was surprised that her English was so .................. as she had never been to England.
    A  definite    B  liquid    C  fluent    D  national

17  He is very stubborn, so it will be difficult to .................. him to go.
    A  persuade    B  suggest    C  make    D  prevent

18  He put a .................. against the tree and climbed up to pick the apples.
    A  scale    B  staircase    C  grade    D  ladder

19  It's six years now since the Socialists came to .................. in that country.
    A  power    B  force    C  control    D  command

20  You're looking very pale — do you .................. sick?
    A  fall    B  faint    C  feel    D  become

[22]

Practice Test 2

21  He stood on one leg, .............. against the wall, while he took off his shoe.
    A stopping    B staying    C leaning    D supporting

22  In a greengrocer's shop there is a lot of .............. when fruit and vegetables are not sold.
    A rot    B waste    C ruin    D rest

23  After the party the children were allowed to finish off the .............. sandwiches and cakes.
    A additional    B leaving    C remaining    D left

24  When the time came to .............. the bill at the hotel she found her purse had been stolen.
    A pay    B pay out    C pay for    D pay up

25  When the manager went to Canada on business his .............. took over all his duties.
    A caretaker    B officer    C deputy    D commander


SECTION B

*In this section you will find after each of the passages a number of questions or unfinished statements about the passage, each with four suggested answers or ways of finishing. You must choose the one which you think fits best.* **On your answer sheet, indicate the letter A, B, C or D against the number of each item 26–40 for the answer you choose.** *Give one answer only to each question. Read each passage right through before choosing your answers.*


FIRST PASSAGE

It was on one of the hottest August days – the fourth, and at twelve o'clock exactly, for a church clock was striking the hour – that a short, heavily-built woman of about fifty, carrying a shopping-bag, came out from the darkness of an old storehouse where she worked every morning as a checker, and set off along the narrow grey street to a bus-stop. Most of the factories and offices in the town were closed for two weeks but the storehouse, which held foodstuffs and other goods that did not keep, had remained open during the holidays. The heat, made worse by the heavy smell of petrol from the main street near by and undisturbed by the slightest current of cooler air, enveloped her. She was neither dressed nor built for energetic activity on a hot day, being very short indeed, and fat, so that she had to roll a little in order to get along. Her tight black dress was worn without a belt or any ornaments other than a large metal cross, well fingered but of no special value, which hung on a

[23]

white ribbon around her neck. Her cracked shoes made loud footsteps in the silence of the empty street of closed buildings. The worn old bag she carried caused her to lean over slightly to her right as she walked, but it was clear that she was used to carrying such heavy weights.

Reaching her usual bus stop, she put down her bag and rested. Then, suddenly conscious of being watched, she turned quickly round and looked sharply upward at the tall man behind her.

He was the only other person waiting, and indeed, at that moment, the only other person in the street. She had never spoken to him, yet his face was already familiar to her: so big, so uncertain, so sweaty. She had seen it yesterday, and the day before, and for all she knew, the day before that as well. For the last three or four days anyway, this great nervous lump of a man, waiting for a bus or hanging about on the footpath outside the storehouse, had become a figure of the street for her; and what was more, a figure of a certain definite type, though she had yet to put her finger on exactly which type it was. More than once, she had felt his interest in her and she had wondered whether he was a policeman.

26  Why were there so few people about in this particular street at midday?
    A  It was too hot to be outside.
    B  Most workers were on holiday.
    C  The lunch-time break had not yet started.
    D  Not many people lived in the area now.

27  What was the woman wearing?
    A  a dark dress with a lot of jewellery
    B  a loose summer dress
    C  a dress with a white collar
    D  a plain and simple dress

28  The woman was hindered in walking by
    A  her tight dress.
    B  her heavy necklace.
    C  her round shape.
    D  her worn-out shoes.

29  The woman turned round because
    A  she heard someone coming.
    B  she thought the bus was due.
    C  she remembered about her bag.
    D  she felt someone looking at her.

30  Why did the woman recognise the man by the bus-stop?
    A  He was the local policeman.
    B  He travelled on the bus regularly.
    C  He had been near the storehouse before.
    D  He was like someone she knew well.

## SECOND PASSAGE

The pig was the last animal to be fully domesticated by the farmer. Unlike the cow and the sheep, it is not a grass-eater. Its ancient home was the forest, where it searched for different kinds of food, such as nuts, roots and dead animals, and found in the bushes protection for its almost hairless body from extremes of sun and cold. For many centuries the farmer allowed it to continue there, leaving his pigs to look after themselves most of the time. As the woodlands began to shrink, the pig slowly began to be kept on the farm itself. But it did not finally come into a shed, where it was fed on waste food from the farm and the house, until the eighteenth century.

The pig, then, became a farm animal in the age of agricultural improvement in Britain in the eighteenth century, but it was given little attention by special animal breeders, for the major farmers of the time preferred to develop the larger kinds of animal. There were, however, various less well-known farmers interested in pigs and they based their improvements on new types of pig from overseas. These were the Chinese pig, and its various relatives, including the Neapolitan pig, which were descended from Chinese pigs that had found their way to the Mediterranean in ancient times. These were very different from the thin and leggy British woodland pigs. They were wider and squarer, with shorter legs and flatter faces, and they matured earlier and produced more delicate meat. By the end of the eighteenth century these overseas pigs had influenced the colour, shape and characteristics of the native British pig a great deal.

In the early nineteenth century, all sorts and conditions of pig-farmer worked at improving all sorts and conditions of pig. Many of the special pigs they developed are now forgotten, but by the end of the century they had established most of the kinds we know in Britain today.

31  In their original wild state pigs
    A  ate the same food as other animals.
    B  wandered across the plains.
    C  lived among trees.
    D  did not go near cows or sheep.

32  Why were pigs not fully domesticated in Britain until the eighteenth century?
    A  They could find food for themselves well enough in woodlands.
    B  There was no suitable food for them on most farms.
    C  It was difficult to develop improved types of pig.
    D  They did not grow well when kept indoors.

33  The passage tells us that in the age of agricultural improvement in Britain in the eighteenth century
    A  very fat pigs were developed.
    B  British types of pig were replaced with overseas ones.
    C  pigs received less attention than other animals.
    D  important breeders concentrated on pigs.

Practice Test 2

34  How did Chinese and Neapolitan pigs differ from native British pigs?
    A  They were taller.
    B  They had shorter noses.
    C  They had stronger legs.
    D  They were rounder.

THIRD PASSAGE

Three friends, Jean, Helen and Emma, have gone on a week's holiday together. They send these three postcards to Ann, who works in the same office.

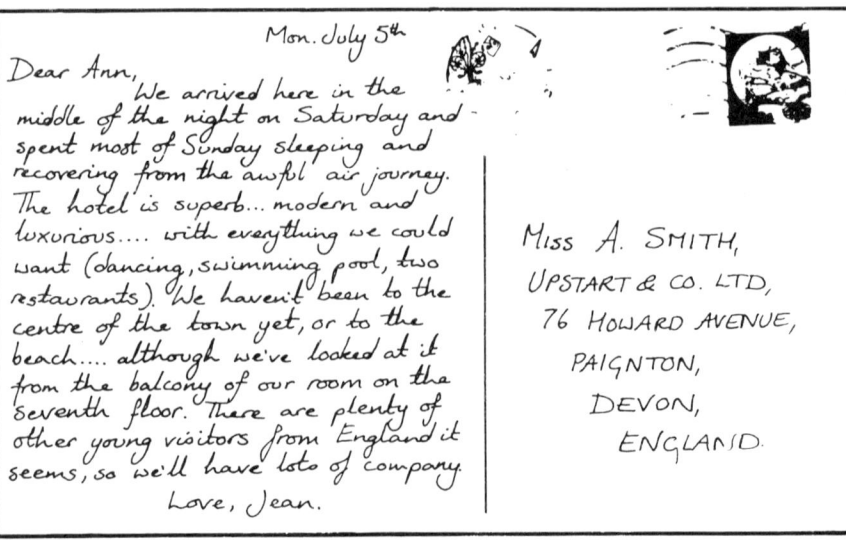

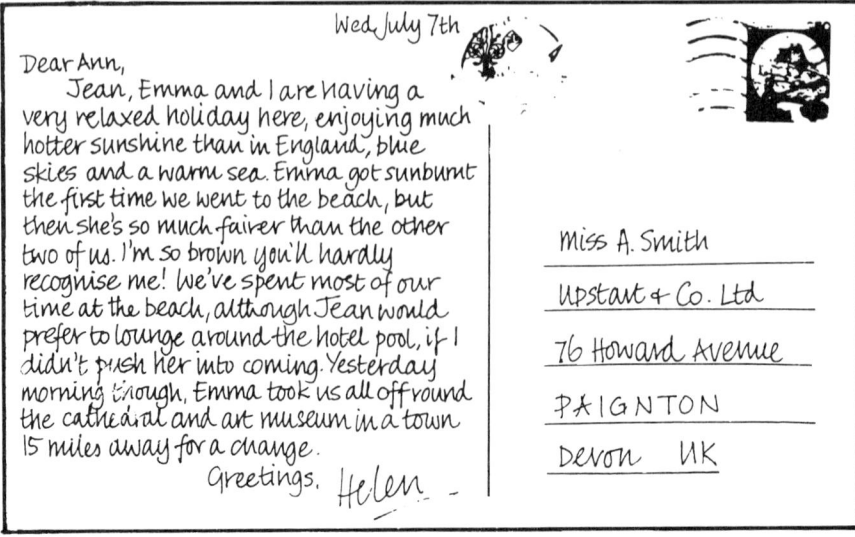

[26]

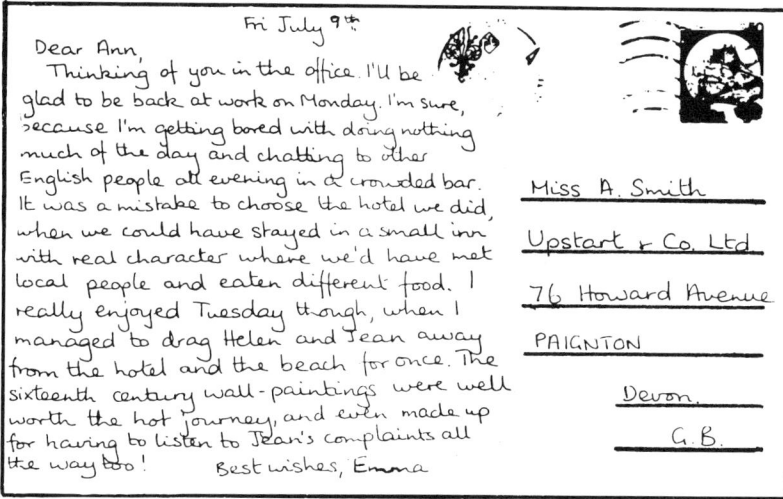

35  Where are the three friends staying?
    A  a modern hotel in the south of England
    B  a large hotel in a seaside town
    C  a small hotel right by the beach
    D  a luxury hotel in an historic town

36  What is the weather like?
    A  too warm for two of them
    B  cool in the evening
    C  too warm for all of them
    D  sunny and hot

37  Which of the three friends seems to get her own way about what they are going to do most of the time?
    A  Jean    B  Helen    C  Emma
    D  no-one more than the others

38  What does Helen most enjoy?
    A  relaxing by the pool
    B  sunbathing on the beach
    C  talking to English people
    D  visiting historic places

39  Who likes the hotel where they are staying the best?
    A  Jean    B  Helen    C  Emma
    D  Two of them like it equally

40  Why will Emma be glad to get back to the office?
    A  the beach is too crowded
    B  the hotel is too expensive
    C  she is finding the holiday dull
    D  she is beginning to dislike Jean and Helen

[27]

*Practice Test 2*

# PAPER 2   COMPOSITION   (1½ hours)

*Write **two only** of the following composition exercises. Your answers must follow exactly the instructions given and must be of between 120 and 180 words each.*

1  You need a job for three months in the summer, and you have seen an advertisement in a newspaper about a temporary job as a tourist guide in your town or city. Write a letter applying for the post.

2  You are looking after some young children. Tell them a story you enjoyed when you were a child.

3  'I woke up and started to cough. The room was full of smoke.' Continue the story, describing your escape from the building.

4  'Most people spend too much time watching television nowadays.' Do you agree?

5  Based on your reading of any one of these books, write on *one* of the following.

JANE AUSTEN: *Sense and Sensibility*
What have you found especially interesting about Jane Austen's attitude to marriage?

G. B. SHAW: *Arms and the Man*
Why does Captain Bluntschli return to the Petkoffs' house after the peace treaty? Explain how this second visit affects the lives of some of the characters in the play.

GRAHAM GREENE: *The Third Man*
'There was something wrong about Lime's death, something the police had been too stupid to discover.' Describe Rollo Martins' attempts to investigate this 'death', until he is proved right by seeing Lime's 'ghost'.

## PAPER 3  USE OF ENGLISH  (2 hours)

1  Fill each of the numbered blanks in the following passage. Use only **one** word in each space.

After we had been marching for two weeks, getting soaked by daily rains and living entirely on the ............(1) we carried with us, we found footprints. Two people were ............(2) of us and travelling fast. We followed ............(3). Each morning, when we ............(4) off again after a night's ............(5), we found their tracks in the forest nearby and ............(6) they had been watching us the ............(7) evening. One night we ............(8) gifts in the forest but they ............(9) not touched. We called out greetings ............(10) the language of the river people but we did not know ............(11) this unknown tribe were able to understand it. In any case ............(12) was no reply. We continued day ............(13) day until eventually we lost all sign of their movements. After three weeks we had almost ............(14) up hope ............(15) making contact. Then early one morning we ............(16) up to find seven men standing within a ............(17) yards of our tent. They were very small and wore nothing ............(18) a wide belt of green leaves ............(19) around their waist. Two of the men had earrings and necklaces made of bones and one carried a woven ............(20) full of roots and fruit.

[29]

*Practice Test 2*

2  Finish each of the following sentences in such a way that it means exactly the same as the sentence printed before it.

    EXAMPLE: I haven't enjoyed myself so much for years.

    ANSWER: It's years *since I enjoyed myself so much.*

a) You can't visit the United States unless you get a visa.
If you don't get a visa you can't visit the United states ✓

b) 'Can I borrow your typewriter, Janet?' asked Peter.
Peter asked if he could borrow her typewriter ✓

c) She started working as a secretary five years ago.
She has been working as a secretary for five years ✓

d) She knows a lot more about it than I do.
I don't know as much about it as she does ✓

e) My French friend finds driving on the left difficult.
My French friend isn't used ~~get use~~ to drive on the left ✗

✗ f) They think the owner of the house is abroad.
The owner of the house must be abroad. ✓

g) We didn't go on holiday because we didn't have enough money.
If we had had enough money we would have gone on holiday. ✓

✗ h) The children couldn't go swimming because the sea was very rough.
The sea was too rough for the children to swimming ✗
that the children couldn't go swimming

i) What a pity you failed your driving test!
I wish you hadn't ~~didn't~~ fail your driving test. ✗

j) The mechanic serviced my car last week.
I had my car serviced last week by the mechanic. ✓

[30]

Practice Test 2

3 Complete each of the following sentences with an appropriate word or phrase made from **time**.

EXAMPLE: I don't like people who arrive late. I'm always *on time*.

a) We found out when the bus left from the ……timetable……

b) Did you get to the station ……in time…… to catch the train?

c) It was 2 a.m. ……by the time [when]…… they had finished tidying up after the party.

d) She wanted to complete the exercise during the lesson but she ran ……out of time……

e) My boyfriend lives in York so I can only visit him from ……time to time……

4 Below are five groups of three words. In the spaces write **one** word which describes each group.

EXAMPLE: Coat, dress, trousers  *clothes*

a) Hammer, screwdriver, saw    ……Tools……

b) Summer, winter, spring    ……Seasons……

c) Lunch, dinner, breakfast    ……meals……

d) Table, chair, bed    ……furniture……

e) Car, bus, lorry    ……vehicles……

5 Make all the changes and additions necessary to produce, from the following sets of words and phrases, sentences which together make a complete letter. Note carefully from the example what kind of alterations need to be made. Write each sentence in the space provided.

EXAMPLE: I / wonder / why you / not / reply / last letter.

ANSWER: I was wondering why you had not replied to my last letter.

[31]

Practice Test 2

Ward 7
Great Northern Hospital
Manchester

Dear Bill,

I / expect / you be surprise / get / letter / me.

a) I expect you are surprised ~~getting~~ a letter ~~to me~~. [to get ... from]
   ~~I expecting you to be~~

As / can see / address above / I be / hospital.

b) As you can see (from) the address above I am in hospital ✓

Last Wednesday / I have / accident / when I drive / work.

c) Last Wednesday I had an accident when I was driving to work. ✓

Child / run out / front / my car / and I / have / stop / sudden / that / car behind / crash / me.

d) A child ran out in front of my car and I had to stop (so) ~~to~~ suddenly that the car behind crashed into me. ✓

Luckily / I wear / seatbelt / so I / not injure badly / although / have / stay / here / next Friday.

e) Luckily I ~~wore~~ [was wearing] my seatbelt so I didn't injure myself badly, although I have to stay here until next Friday. ✓

It be / very boring / I be pleased / see / if you / have / spare time.

f) It is going to be very boring (so) I would be pleased to see you if you have a bit of spare time. ✓

Visiting hours / be / 7.00 to 9.00 / evening.

g) The visiting hours are from 7.00 to 9.00 in the evening. ✓

I hope / able / come.

h) I hope you (will be) are able to come. ✓

Give my regards to your family.

Yours,
John

[32]

6  Susan Bates and Janet Peel are going to move to London to study at a college there. Susan has come to London before the term starts to look for a flat for them both. She has visited four flats and is writing a letter to Janet to tell her about them. Look at the notes Susan made about each flat and then complete her letter.

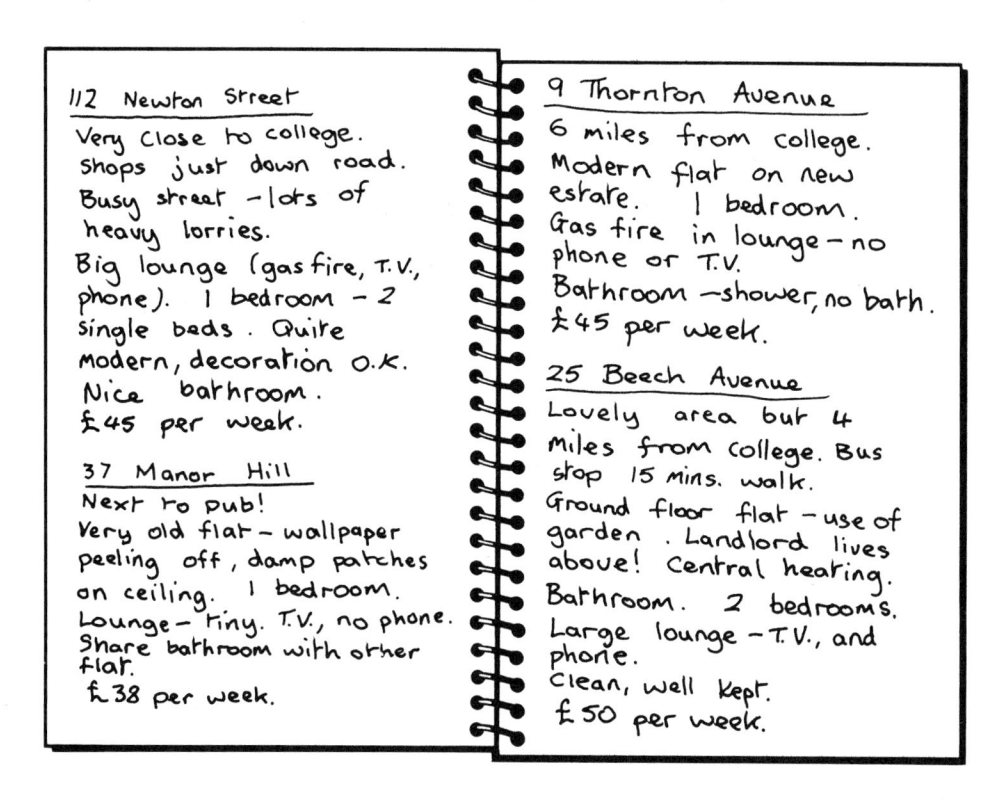

---

**112 Newton Street**
Very close to college. Shops just down road. Busy street – lots of heavy lorries. Big lounge (gas fire, T.V., phone). 1 bedroom – 2 single beds. Quite modern, decoration O.K. Nice bathroom.
£45 per week.

**37 Manor Hill**
Next to pub! Very old flat – wallpaper peeling off, damp patches on ceiling. 1 bedroom. Lounge – tiny. T.V., no phone. Share bathroom with other flat.
£38 per week.

**9 Thornton Avenue**
6 miles from college. Modern flat on new estate. 1 bedroom. Gas fire in lounge – no phone or T.V. Bathroom – shower, no bath.
£45 per week.

**25 Beech Avenue**
Lovely area but 4 miles from college. Bus stop 15 mins. walk. Ground floor flat – use of garden. Landlord lives above! Central heating. Bathroom. 2 bedrooms. Large lounge – T.V., and phone. Clean, well kept.
£50 per week.

---

Dear Janet,

Just a quick letter to tell you what I've been doing. I went to see four flats today and I liked one of them very much. It was in a road called ........................ and I think it would suit us very well because

..............................................................................................................

..............................................................................................................

..............................................................................................................

..............................................................................................................

However it did have a couple of drawbacks. ............................................

There was another flat in ........................... which was nearly as good.

I don't think it would be as suitable for us as the other one because

One of the flats I saw was really dreadful. I'm amazed the landlord wanted so much for it. I doubt if you'd even consider living there because ...........................

I'd better finish so that I can post this. Ring me as soon as you can and let me know what you think so I can make all the arrangements.

> Yours,
>
> Susan

Practice Test 2

# PAPER 4  LISTENING COMPREHENSION
(about 30 minutes)

### FIRST PART

*For questions 1–7 fill in the gaps in the following information sheet.*

*Permitted clothing* (1) .................................................. and bathing costume
*Best time of year:* July, August, September
*Best time of day:* An hour and half after (2) ..................................................
*Style of swimming:* any style acceptable
*Total training:* should take at least (3) .................................................. months. You should build up your training, using the following as a rough guide: two-hour swims, morning and evening, followed by six-hour swims, and then ten-hour swims; and finally, in your last three weeks a minimum of (4) .................................................. hours swimming per week should be your aim.

*Basic Rules*
Only lanolin (5) .................................................. may be used as a protection against cold
Taking food and drink is (6) .................................................., but on no account must you touch or hang on to the boat, as this means (7) ..................................................

[35]

*Practice Test 2*

## SECOND PART

For questions 8–12 tick (√) one of the boxes A, B, C or D.

8  Mr Harding serves the customer because
   A  the customer wants to speak to him.
   B  the first assistant works in another department.
   C  the first assistant is too busy.
   D  the customer knows him.

   A
   B
   C
   D

9  The customer wants to change the cassette because it
   A  has a crack in it.
   B  has caused a fault in his cassette player.
   C  has a part missing.
   D  will not work in his cassette player.

   A
   B
   C
   D

10 Mr Harding suggests that the customer is to blame because
   A  he is using the cassette in someone else's machine.
   B  the customer's machine is old.
   C  the cassette needs repairing.
   D  nobody else has made a similar complaint.

   A
   B
   C
   D

11 Mr Harding says he won't change the cassette because
   A  the shop's rule is not to change cassettes.
   B  the customer has damaged the cassette.
   C  he believes the cassette came from another shop.
   D  he believes there is nothing really wrong with it.

   A
   B
   C
   D

12 Why doesn't the manager speak to the customer?
   A  He's at lunch.
   B  He's got the whole day off.
   C  He's serving someone else.
   D  He's at a meeting.

   A
   B
   C
   D

[36]

## THIRD PART

*A learner driver comes across various difficulties. In the boxes numbered 13–16 enter the letter for each difficulty in the order in which they happen. The first one has been done for you.*

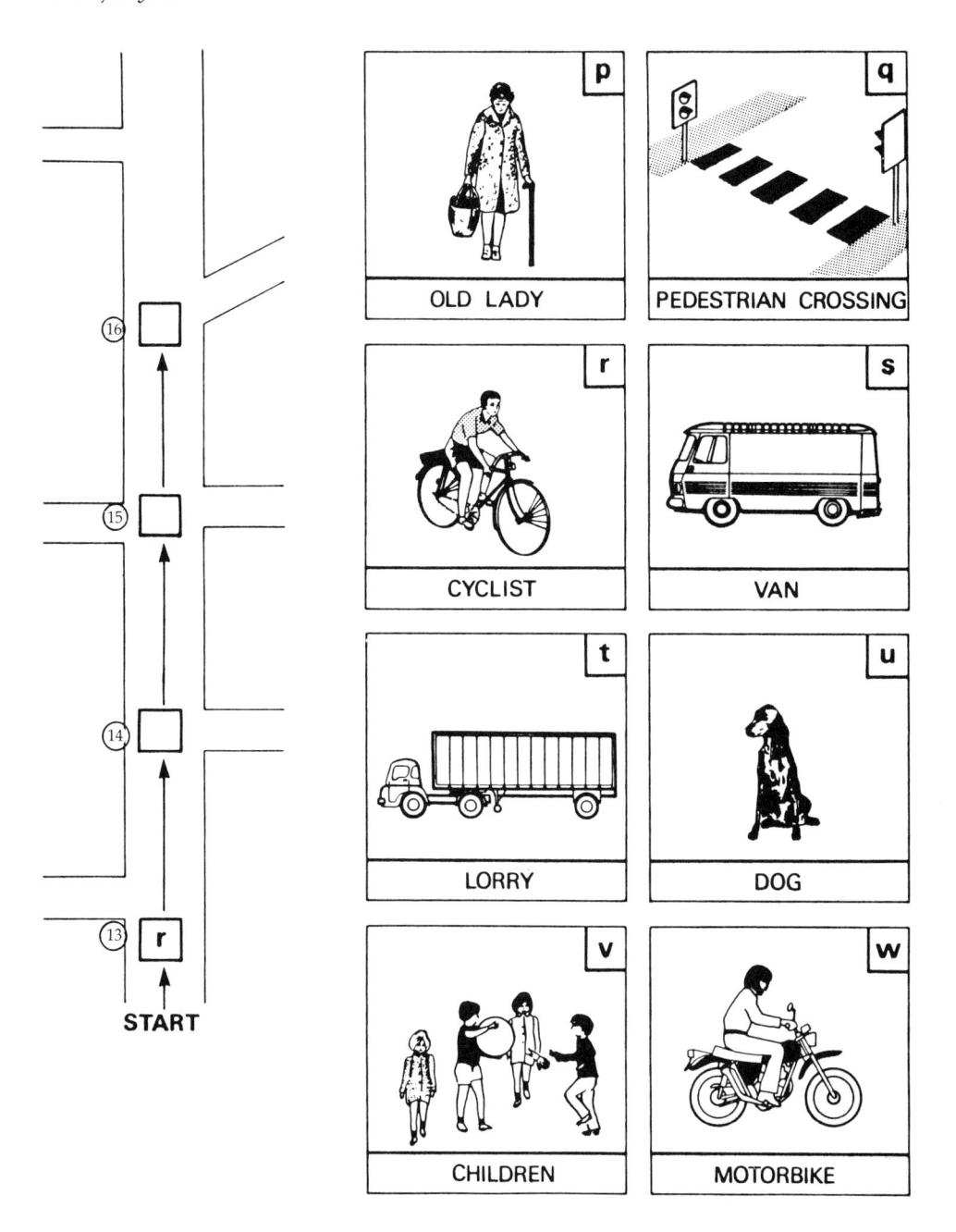

| | |
|---|---|
| **p** OLD LADY | **q** PEDESTRIAN CROSSING |
| **r** CYCLIST | **s** VAN |
| **t** LORRY | **u** DOG |
| **v** CHILDREN | **w** MOTORBIKE |

*Practice Test 2*

## FOURTH PART

For questions 17–26 fill in the details about what there is to see and do in Stratford-upon-Avon, where Shakespeare was born.

Shakespeare Centre. Address: Henley Street ............

(17) Details of Shakespearian Houses. Phone number: Stratford-upon-Avon ............

(18) World of Shakespeare Theatre. Length of show ............

(19) Harvard House. Address: ............

(20) ............ Museum Address: Shakespeare Street.

(21) Details of Guided tours: Phone number: Stratford-upon-Avon ............

Royal Shakespeare Theatre. Phone number: Stratford-upon-Avon 295623

(22) 1st January: Sale of old ............

(23) Time from 10:30 a.m. to ............

(24) 6th–8th January: 'The Land of Make-Believe', at Shottery Memorial ............

Tourist Information Centre. Opening hours

(25) From: ............

To: 5:00 p.m.

(26) Closed on ............

Phone Stratford-upon-Avon 293127

*Practice Test 2*

## PAPER 5  INTERVIEW  (about 15 minutes)

You will be asked to take part in a conversation with a group of other students or with your teacher. The conversation will be based on one particular topic area or theme, for example holidays, work, food.

Of course each interview will be different for each student or group of students, but a *typical* interview is described below.

* At the start of the interview you will be asked to talk about one of the photographs among the Interview Exercises at the back of the book.

* You will then be asked to discuss one of the passages at the back of the book. Your teacher may ask you to talk about its content, where you think it comes from, who the author or speaker is, whether you agree or disagree with it, and so on. You will *not* be asked to read the passage aloud, but you may quote parts of it to make your point.

* You may then be asked to discuss for example an advertisement, a leaflet, extract from a newspaper etc. Your teacher will tell you which of the Interview Exercises to look at.

* You may also be asked to take part in an activity with a group of other students or your teacher. Your teacher will tell you which section among the Interview Exercises you should look at.

# Practice Test 3

## PAPER 1   READING COMPREHENSION   (1 hour)

*Answer all questions. Indicate your choice of answer in every case* **on the separate answer sheet** *already given out, which should show your name and examination index number. Follow carefully the instructions about how to record your answers. Give* **one answer only** *to each question. Marks will not be deducted for wrong answers: your total score on this test will be the number of correct answers you give.*

### SECTION A

*In this section you must choose the word or phrase which best completes each sentence.* **On your answer sheet** *indicate the letter A, B, C or D against the number of each item 1 to 25 for the word or phrase you choose.*

1  The blue curtains began to ............ after they had been hanging in the sun for two months.
   A  fade     B  die     C  dissolve     D  melt

2  Learners of English as a foreign language often fail to ............ between unfamiliar sounds in that language.
   A  separate     B  differ     C  distinguish     D  solve

3  The wind blew so hard and so strongly that the windows ............ in their frames.
   A  rattled     B  slapped     C  flapped     D  shocked

4  I have lived near the railway for so long now that I've grown ............ to the noise of the trains.
   A  accustomed     B  familiar     C  unconscious     D  aware

5  In spite of her protests, her father ............ her train for the race three hours a day.
   A  let     B  made     C  insisted     D  caused

6  It was impossible for her to tell the truth so she had to ............ a story.
   A  invent     B  combine     C  manage     D  lie

7  The car had a ............ tyre, so we had to change the wheel.
   A  broken     B  cracked     C  bent     D  flat

[40]

8  She applied for training as a pilot, but they turned her .......... because of her poor eyesight.
   A back   B up   C over   D down

9  The only feature .......... to these two flowers is their preference for sandy soil.
   A similar   B same   C shared   D common

10 The play was very long, but there were two ............ .
   A intervals   B rests   C interruptions   D gaps

11 These old houses are going to be .......... soon.
   A laid out   B run down   C pulled down   D knocked out

12 She rang to make an early .......... at the hairdressers.
   A order   B date   C assignment   D appointment

13 The law states that heavy goods delivery vehicles may not carry .......... of more than fifteen tons.
   A masses   B sizes   C measures   D loads

14 The young soldier .......... a dangerous mission across the desert, although he knew that he might be killed.
   A undertook   B agreed   C promised   D entered

15 You must .......... that your safety belt is fastened.
   A examine   B secure   C check   D guarantee

16 He .......... a rare disease when he was working in the hospital.
   A took   B suffered   C infected   D caught

17 My sister had a baby daughter yesterday, and she is my first ............ .
   A nephew   B cousin   C niece   D relation

18 When he heard the joke, he burst into loud ............ .
   A smiles   B laughter   C amusement   D enjoyment

19 The traffic lights .......... to green, and the cars drove on.
   A exchanged   B turned   C removed   D shone

20 It is a good idea to be .......... dressed when you go for an interview.
   A finely   B boldly   C smartly   D clearly

21 If we go to the market we might find a ............ .
   A trade   B shopping   C chance   D bargain

*Practice Test 3*

22  If he drinks any more beer, I don't think he'll be .............. to play this afternoon.
    A skilled    B capable    C possible    D fit

23  That's a nice coat, and the colour .............. you well.
    A fits    B matches    C shows    D suits

24  Many accidents in the home could be .............. if householders gave more thought to safety in their houses.
    A avoided    B excluded    C protected    D preserved

25  Smoking is a very bad habit, which many people find difficult to ...............
    A break    B beat    C breathe    D cough

**SECTION B**

*In this section you will find after each of the passages a number of questions or unfinished statements about the passage, each with four suggested answers or ways of finishing. You must choose the one which you think fits best.* **On your answer sheet, indicate the letter A, B, C, or D against the number of each item 26–40 for the answer you choose. Give one answer only to each question. Read each passage right through before choosing your answers.**

FIRST PASSAGE

Through a series of experiments an American scientist has obtained an understanding of the social structure of the most complex of ant societies. The ants examined are the only creatures other than man to have given up hunting and collecting for a completely agricultural way of life. In their underground nests they cultivate gardens on soil made from finely chopped leaves. This is a complex operation requiring considerable division of labour. The workers of this type of ant can be divided into four groups according to size. Each of the groups performs a particular set of jobs.

The making and care of the gardens and the nursing of the young ants are done by the smallest workers. Slightly larger workers are responsible for chopping up leaves to make them suitable for use in the gardens and for cleaning the nest. A third group of still larger ants do the construction work and collect fresh leaves from outside the nest. The largest are the soldier ants, responsible for defending the nest.

To find out how good the various size-groups are at different tasks, the scientist measured the amount of work done by the ants against the amount of energy they used. He examined first the gathering and carrying of leaves. He selected one of the size-groups, and then measured how efficiently these ants could find leaves and run back to the nest. Then he repeated the experiment for each of the other size-groups. In this way he could see whether any group could do the job more efficiently than the group normally undertaking it.

The intermediate-sized ants that normally perform this task proved to be the most efficient for their energy costs, but when the scientist examined the whole set of jobs performed by each group of ants it appeared that some sizes of worker ant were not ideally suited to the particular jobs they performed.

26 In which way are the ants different from other non-human societies?
   A  They do not need to search for food.
   B  They do not need to look for shelter.
   C  Individuals vary in social status.
   D  Individuals perform different functions.

27 It seems that smaller ants perform more of the
   A  construction tasks.
   B  domestic tasks.
   C  defensive work.
   D  heavy work.

28 "Good" (first line of third paragraph) refers to the ants'
   A  co-operation in working.
   B  sense of responsibility.
   C  efficiency in working.
   D  willingness to work hard.

29 The scientist's work was based on
   A  occasional observations.
   B  systematic observations.
   C  observations of several nests.
   D  observations of an undisturbed nest.

30 The organization of the ants has the effect of
   A  getting the most work done.
   B  dividing the work up systematically.
   C  each ant helping with all the tasks.
   D  each ant doing what it can do best.

## SECOND PASSAGE

Let children learn to judge their own work. A child learning to talk does not learn by being corrected all the time: if corrected too much, he will stop talking. He notices a thousand times a day the difference between the language he uses and the language those around him use. Bit by bit, he makes the necessary changes to make his language like other people's. In the same way, children learning to do all the other things they learn to do without being taught – to walk, run, climb, whistle, ride a bicycle – compare their own performances with those of more skilled people, and slowly make the needed changes. But in school we never give a child a chance to find out his mistakes for himself, let alone correct them. We do it all for him. We act as if we thought that he would never notice a mistake unless it was pointed out to him, or correct it unless he was made to. Soon he becomes dependent on the teacher. Let him do it himself. Let him work out, with the help of other children if he wants it, what this word says, what the answer is to that problem, whether this is a good way of saying or doing this or not.

If it is a matter of right answers, as it may be in mathematics or science, give him the answer book. Let him correct his own papers. Why should we teachers waste time on such routine work? Our job should be to help the child when he tells us that he can't find the way to get the right answer. Let's end all this nonsense of grades, exams, marks. Let us throw them all out, and let the children learn what all educated persons must some day learn, how to measure their own understanding, how to know what they know or do not know.

Let them get on with this job in the way that seems most sensible to them, with our help as school teachers if they ask for it. The idea that there is a body of knowledge to be learnt at school and used for the rest of one's life is nonsense in a world as complicated and rapidly changing as ours. Anxious parents and teachers say, 'But suppose they fail to learn something essential, something they will need to get on in the world?' Don't worry! If it is essential, they will go out into the world and learn it.

31  What does the author think is the best way for children to learn things?
  A  by copying what other people do
  B  by making mistakes and having them corrected
  C  by listening to explanations from skilled people
  D  by asking a great many questions

32  What does the author think teachers do which they should not do?
  A  They give children correct answers.
  B  They point out children's mistakes to them.
  C  They allow children to mark their own work.
  D  They encourage children to copy from one another.

33  The passage suggests that learning to speak and learning to ride a bicycle are
    A  not really important skills.
    B  more important than other skills.
    C  basically different from learning adult skills.
    D  basically the same as learning other skills.

34  Exams, grades and marks should be abolished because children's progress should only be estimated by
    A  educated persons.
    B  the children themselves.
    C  teachers.
    D  parents.

35  The author fears that children will grow up into adults who are
    A  too independent of others.
    B  too critical of themselves.
    C  unable to think for themselves.
    D  unable to use basic skills.

THIRD PASSAGE

# CAR HIRE

Hiring a self-drive car really adds to the enjoyment of your holiday. There are so many interesting places to visit, and if you enjoy seeing more than just the city centre there's no better way to explore than by car.

## HIRE CHARGES

**What's included**
(a) Unlimited mileage.
(b) Expenses on oil, maintenance and repairs, which will be repaid on production of receipts.
(c) Full insurance cover but exclusive of personal accident (see below) and contents.

**What's not included**
(a) Personal accident insurance.
(b) Garaging, petrol, parking and traffic fines.

## CONDITIONS OF HIRE

1. The minimum rental period at these special low prices is three days. For prices for periods of one or two days only see our representative at the hotel.
2. Car hire **must** be booked six weeks or more before arrival in London to guarantee a car. But if you have been unable to make a booking in advance please see our representative at the hotel who may still be able to help you.
3. The car types specified on the sheet are examples of the type of vehicles available in each price range, but a particular car cannot be guaranteed.

Upon delivery the driver(s) will be asked to sign the car hire company's Conditions of Hire.

If you decide to hire a car, just fill in the Booking Form and return it to us. A booking fee of £12 as part of the car hire cost is required.

Should you be forced to cancel your car hire booking after payment in full (two weeks before date of hire), a cancellation charge of £12 will be made.

36  What costs is a car hirer responsible for?
   A  insurance against damage to the car
   B  insurance against injury to the driver
   C  the cost of maintenance of the car
   D  the cost of repairs to the car

37  The rates for car hire are especially cheap when
    A  two days are booked.
    B  three days are booked.
    C  the booking is made in London.
    D  the booking is made from outside Britain.

38  The cost of oil
    A  has to be paid by the driver.
    B  should be charged to the company.
    C  is covered by the insurance payment.
    D  can be reclaimed by the driver.

39  What does the hire charge for a three day period depend on?
    A  the classification of the car
    B  the distance travelled
    C  the cost of oil and petrol
    D  the cost of garaging

40  If car hirers change their minds after paying the whole cost of hiring, the £12 booking fee is
    A  returned in part immediately.
    B  not returned at all.
    C  not required.
    D  returned in full within six weeks.

## PAPER 2  COMPOSITION  (1½ hours)

*Write **two only** of the following composition exercises. Your answers must follow exactly the instructions given and must be of between 120 and 180 words each.*

1 The radio-cassette recorder you bought recently is not working properly. Write the letter you would send with the recorder to the manufacturers, explaining the fault and asking them to repair it.

2 Imagine you are the mayor of your local town. Write a speech to welcome a group of foreign schoolchildren and their teachers who are visiting your town.

3 Describe a journey (by land, sea or air) on which you met a particularly unpleasant person.

4 'Much stricter punishments would soon reduce the amount of crime.' What is your opinion?

5 Based on your reading of any one of these books, write on *one* of the following.

   JANE AUSTEN: *Sense and Sensibility*
   'Mr Willoughby has not behaved as a gentleman should.' What had Willoughby done to make Elinor think so badly of him?

   G. B. SHAW: *Arms and the Man*
   What are Captain Bluntschli's views on war?

   GRAHAM GREENE: *The Third Man*
   What sort of man was Rollo Martins and why did he go to Vienna?

# PAPER 3  USE OF ENGLISH  (2 hours)

1  *Fill each of the numbered blanks in the following passage. Use only **one** word in each space.*

The two women were standing now on the deck of the steamer looking at the riverside scene. To the left lay a .................. (1) of small boats .................. (2) the landing stage. Behind .................. (3) the smooth white fronts of the hotels .................. (4) above the yellow city walls. Straight ahead was .................. (5) Ellie had brought her to .................. (6): a line of flat boats with a wooden walkway laid .................. (7) it, crowded at .................. (8) evening hour .................. (9) country people returning from market. This made .................. (10) truly fascinating sight. They .................. (11) see the brightly- .................. (12) skirts of the women and the bundles on the backs of the men .................. (13) they moved towards the .................. (14) shore. Working .................. (15) way against them was a .................. (16) of soldiers coming down .................. (17) the castle to spend the evening in the town. .................. (18) a gun sounded from the bank .................. (19) them both to start and hold .................. (20) other's hands more tightly.

[49]

Practice Test 3

2   Finish each of the following sentences in such a way that it means exactly the same as the sentence printed before it.

EXAMPLE: I haven't enjoyed myself so much for years.
ANSWER: It's years *since I enjoyed myself so much.*

a) I'm always nervous when I travel by air.
Travelling by air makes me always nervous.

b) He could not afford to buy the car.
The car was so expensive that he couldn't afford to buy it.

c) 'Why don't you put your luggage under the seat?' he asked.
He suggested him to put his luggage under the seat.

d) Although he had a good salary, he was unhappy in his job.
In spite of having a good salary, he was unhappy in his job.

e) He was annoyed because his secretary came late to work.
He objected that his secretary came late to work.

f) I'm sorry I missed your birthday party.
I wish I didn't miss your birthday party.

g) They haven't cleaned the streets this week.
The streets haven't been cleaned this week (by them).

h) Apples are usually cheaper than oranges.
Apples are not more expensive than oranges usually.

i) I advise you to put your money in the bank.
You'd would be well advise to put your money in the bank.

j) That restaurant is so dirty that no one wants to eat there.
It is such dirty restaurant that no one wants to eat there.

[50]

Practice Test 3

3  In each of the following sentences there is a blank with a word just before it. Fill each blank with a word that combines with the one given in a way that fits the sentence.

EXAMPLE: He paid a lot of money for his first- *class* ticket.

a) She hasn't much money to spend because she can find only a part- *time* job.

b) John always wears very well- *cleaned* shoes.

c) He looks rather severe but he is really a very kind- *old* man.

d) People often put on weight when they become middle- *aged*.

e) My mother always gives her guests home- *made* cakes for tea.

4  Fill each blank with a phrase made from **go**.

EXAMPLE: The price of petrol has *gone up* from 40p to 50p per litre.

a) You will have to *go over* your homework again because it's full of mistakes.

b) When the tide *goes back* there's plenty of sand to sit on. (marea)

c) The milk smells horrible. It must have *gone off*, so you will have to put lemon in your tea.

d) As two of the staff here have *gone down* with flu, we can't finish the work today.

e) She swims so well that she really should *go in* the competition.

[51]

Practice Test 3

5 *In the following conversation, the parts numbered (1) to (6) have been left out. Complete them suitably.*

A  Worldwide Travel Services—Can I help you?

B  Yes, thank you. I would like to go to New York as soon as possible. When (1) is it the first ticket available ?

A  There will be a flight tomorrow at 12.15.

B  Are there any seats for this flight ?

A  Yes, Sir. The flight is not yet fully booked.

B  What (3) is the price for a first class single ticket ?

A  A first-class single ticket is £315.

B  Can (4) you book two tickets for this flight ?

A  Certainly, Sir. Two first-class tickets for flight number CX202.

B  When (5) can I go to pick the tickets up ?

A  If you come to my office after 4 p.m. today I will have them ready for you.

B  Only one more thing. How (6) can I go to the hotel in N.Y ?

A  We can send a car to your hotel or you can reserve seats in our private coach.

[52]

6  *The following four people are travelling on a train, reading different newspapers or magazines. Using the information given, continue paragraphs 1–4 on page 54 in about 50 words each.*

| Name | Age | Family | Job | Interests |
|---|---|---|---|---|
| Mary Brown | 45 | Married. 2 children, John (garage mechanic) Sandra (at Secretarial College). | Assistant in dress shop. | Making clothes for herself and daughter. Knitting. Collecting pictures of the Queen which she sticks into a book. Gossiping with friends about television and film stars. |
| James Moore | 52 | Married. 2 sons, both in family business. | Buying and selling houses. | Anything to do with making money. Owns large country house and likes buying things to make it more beautiful. Shooting and fishing. |
| Frank Smith | 23 | Single. Lives with parents in small town. | Railway clerk. | Football and swimming. Spends summer holidays in Spain and Portugal near hot, sandy beaches. Likes spending his evenings with his friends and going to discos. |
| Anne Jones | 28 | Recently married to a biologist. | College lecturer. | Playing the piano. Going to opera and concerts. Active member of local political group. Likes discussing woman's place in the modern world. Entertaining friends to dinner. |

| People's Daily | Economic News | MODERN SOCIETY | POPULAR OPINION |
|---|---|---|---|
| ★Sandra's Friend the Elephant  ★Disco Beat Latest (Mick's new album)  ★Win your next great Mediterranean sun holiday  ★3 pages of Sportsnews | Pound/Dollar—Latest fears  Investment Advice  This week's special features on  COUNTRY SPORTS  ANTIQUE FURNITURE | —Zambia-Progress Report  —Secretary or Career Woman?  —Chopin Festival  —International Cookery Series— Part 14 | Royal Babies —delightful picture series  On with the Old Love —Patricia explains  Fashion at your fingertips —useful ideas |

[53]

(1) *I think Mary Brown is reading*

(2) *James Moore has chosen*

(3) *Frank Smith prefers*

(4) *Anne Jones is the sort of woman who reads*

*Practice Test 3*

# PAPER 4  LISTENING COMPREHENSION
(about 30 minutes)

FIRST PART

*Put a tick (√) against the two men Mary Brown describes.*

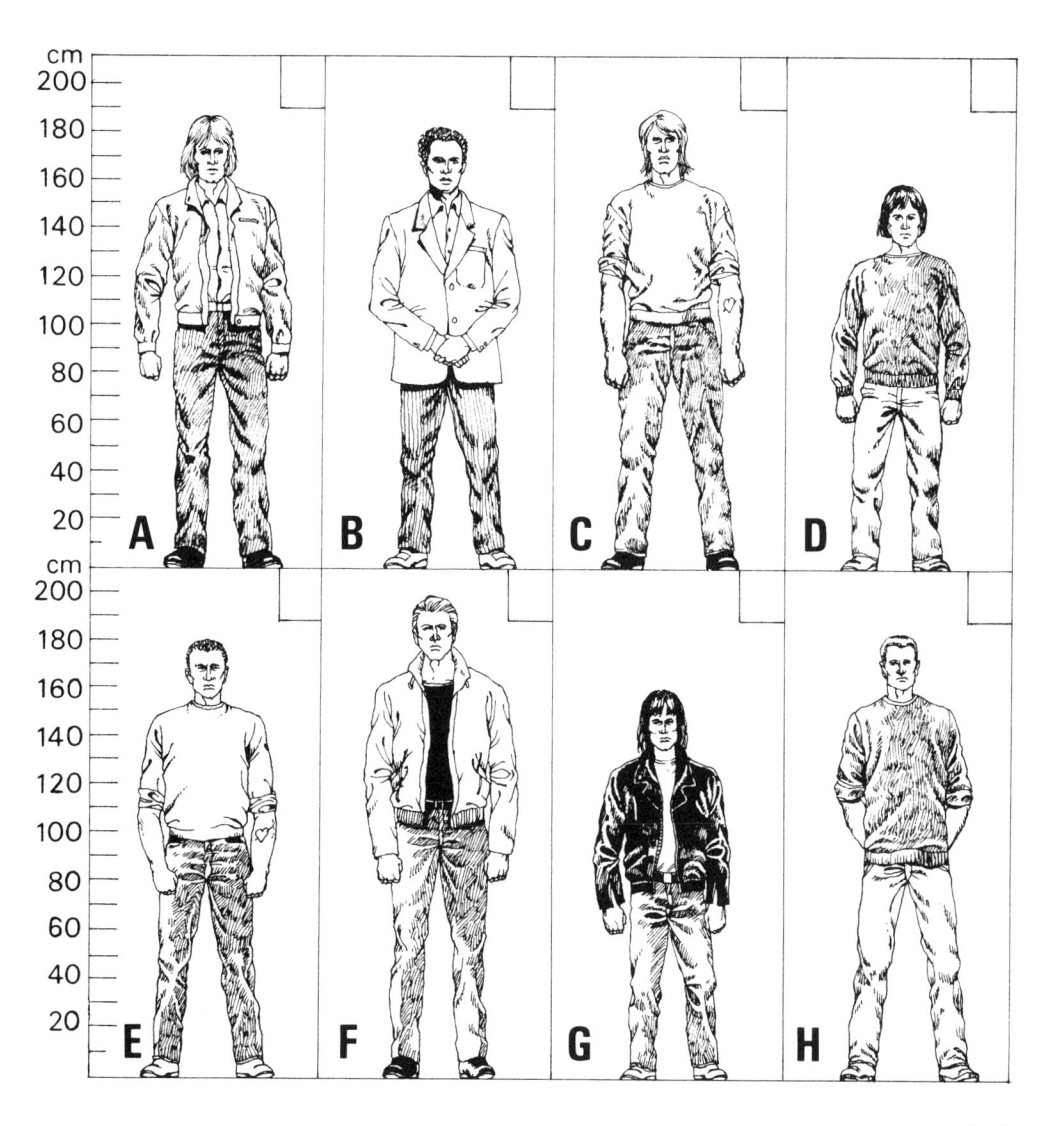

[55]

Practice Test 3

## SECOND PART

*For questions 2–14, fill in the missing information in the messages which Mrs Davis wrote for her husband after listening to the answering machine. The missing information you supply should be as brief as possible.*

---

13th March

Mrs Curry (tel no ......................................................... (2)
wants you to mend her ............................................... (3)


Mr Harris rang.
He sounded slightly ..................................................... (4)
Can you go and mend his ........................................... (5)
Please either ................................................................ (6)
OR ring his neighbour (tel no .............................. ) (7)


Miss Embury rang to ................................................... (8)
not being there when you called.
Can you tell her how much it would cost ...............
........................................................................? (9)
Her tel no is ................................................................. (10)


Mr Grant (tel no ...................................................... ) (11)
would like you to ............................................... him (12)
about his ..................................................................... (13)
His address is .......................... Station Avenue.    (14)

---

[56]

Practice Test 3

THIRD PART

For questions 15–19 put a tick (✓) in the box which corresponds to the man's answers.

15  Does he usually go abroad for summer holidays?

| Yes | |
|---|---|
| No | |

16  Where did he go last year?

| A | Italy | |
|---|---|---|
| B | Corfu | |
| C | Majorca | |
| D | France | |

17  How long did he go away for last year?

| A | 1 week | |
|---|---|---|
| B | 2 weeks | |
| C | 3 weeks | |

18  Where does he plan to go this year?

| A | nowhere | |
|---|---|---|
| B | same place as last year | |
| C | not certain | |
| D | Asia | |

*Practice Test 3*

19  Why does he say he will have a holiday this year?

| A | He likes to get a suntan |  |
|---|---|---|
| B | He likes to travel |  |
| C | He deserves a holiday |  |
| D | His friends have asked him |  |

*For questions 20–22 tick the box which corresponds to the woman's answers.*

20  Did she enjoy her holiday last year?

| Yes |  |
|---|---|
| No |  |

21  Where did she say she might go this year?

| A | Italy |  |
|---|---|---|
| B | France |  |
| C | Greece |  |
| D | Majorca |  |

22  How does she decide where to go on holiday?

| A | friend's recommendation |  |
|---|---|---|
| B | where the weather is good |  |
| C | on a sudden idea |  |
| D | by long-term planning |  |

## PAPER 5  INTERVIEW   (about 15 minutes)

You will be asked to take part in a conversation with a group of other students or with your teacher. The conversation will be based on one particular topic area or theme, for example holidays, work, food.

Of course each interview will be different for each student or group of students, but a *typical* interview is described below.

* At the start of the interview you will be asked to talk about one of the photographs among the Interview Exercises at the back of the book.

* You will then be asked to discuss one of the passages at the back of the book. Your teacher may ask you to talk about its content, where you think it comes from, who the author or speaker is, whether you agree or disagree with it, and so on. You will *not* be asked to read the passage aloud, but you may quote parts of it to make your point.

* You may then be asked to discuss for example an advertisement, a leaflet, extract from a newspaper etc. Your teacher will tell you which of the Interview Exercises to look at.

* You may also be asked to take part in an activity with a group of other students or your teacher. Your teacher will tell you which section among the Interview Exercises you should look at.

# Practice Test 4

## PAPER 1   READING COMPREHENSION   (1 hour)

*Answer all questions. Indicate your choice of answer in every case* **on the separate answer sheet** *already given out, which should show your name and examination index number. Follow carefully the instructions about how to record your answers. Give* **one answer only** *to each question. Marks will not be deducted for wrong answers: your total score on this test will be related to the number of correct answers you give.*

### SECTION A

*In this section you must choose the word or phrase which best completes each sentence.* **On your answer sheet** *indicate the letter, A, B, C or D, against the number of each item 1 to 25, for the word or phrase you choose.*

1  After the water workers went on strike there was a .................. of water.
   A drain    B shortage    C loss    D decrease

2  As the streets of our cities become busier, people are turning more and more to the .................. bicycle.
   A historical    B old-fashioned    C old-aged    D elderly

3  .................. it was raining heavily he went out without a raincoat.
   A In spite    B In spite of    C However    D Although

4  As far as I'm .................., it's quite all right for you to leave early.
   A concerned    B regarded    C consulted    D bothered

5  I expect it will rain again when we're on holiday this year, but at least we are properly prepared .................. it this time.
   A about    B at    C with    D for

6  If only he .................. told us the truth in the first place, things wouldn't have gone so wrong.
   A had    B has    C would have    D should have

7  I know him by .................., but I have no idea what his name is.
   A sight    B myself    C heart    D chance

8  No child .................. the age of sixteen will be admitted to this film.
   A before    B except    C lacking    D below

[60]

9   Mr Smith was .............. in a road accident.
    A wronged    B wounded    C injured    D damaged

10  Is it worth waiting for a table at this restaurant or shall we go .............. else?
    A anywhere    B otherwise    C somewhere    D everywhere

11  The picture is ..............; the thief will be most disappointed when he tries to sell it!
    A priceless    B invalid    C unprofitable    D worthless

12  I am not sure, but .............. I know he has decided to accept the new job in London.
    A according    B on the whole    C as far as    D as long as

13  I can't .............. what he's doing; it's so dark down there.
    A see through    B make out    C look into    D show up

14  Do you know what time the train .............. to Birmingham?
    A reaches    B gets    C arrives    D comes

15  Having looked the place .............., the gang went away to make their plans.
    A through    B over    C down    D out

16  When we came back from holiday our suitcases were .............. by the Customs Officers.
    A guarded    B tested    C corrected    D examined

17  The child was so noisy that his mother told him not to be such a .............. .
    A nuisance    B trouble    C bother    D worry

18  The junior Minister's remarks on television about the strike .............. the Prime Minister so much that he was sacked.
    A disordered    B disliked    C disagreed    D displeased

19  Could you be more specific about what is .............. in this particular job?
    A enclosed    B concentrated    C presented    D involved

20  We went to see the play last night and, .............. for Tony, we all enjoyed it very much.
    A apart    B aside    C except    D unless

21  They haven't beaten me yet. I still have one or two .............. up my sleeve.
    A traps    B tricks    C jokes    D defences

22  You .............. go to the dentist's before your toothache gets worse.
    A ought to    B ought    C rather    D better

[61]

Practice Test 4

23  According to the forecast it will be mostly cloudy, with .................. of rain in the north.
    A  outbreaks    B  elements    C  bursts    D  times

24  .................. of all of us who are here tonight, I would like to thank Mr Jones for his talk.
    A  On behalf    B  On account    C  In person    D  Instead

25  The brothers are so alike I cannot .................. one from the other.
    A  say    B  notice    C  mark    D  tell

## SECTION B

*In this section you will find after each of the passages a number of questions or unfinished statements about the passage, each with four suggested answers or ways of finishing. You must choose the one which you think fits best.* **On your answer sheet,** *indicate the letter A, B, C or D against the number of each item 26–40 for the answer you choose. Read each passage right through before choosing your answers.*

## FIRST PASSAGE

England's highest main-line railway station hangs on to life by a thread: deserted and unmanned since it was officially closed in 1970, Dent, situated high in the hills of Yorkshire, wakes up on six summer weekends each year, when a special charter train unloads walkers, sightseers and people who simply want to catch a train from the highest station, on to its platforms.

But even this limited existence may soon be brought to an end. Dent station is situated on the Settle to Carlisle railway line, said to be the most scenic in the country. But no amount of scenic beauty can save the line from British Rail's cash problems. This year, for the sake of economy, the express trains which used to pass through Dent station have been put on to another route.

It is now an open secret that British Rail sees no future for this railway line. Most of its trains disappeared some time ago. Its bridge, built on a grand scale a century ago, is falling down. It is not alone. Half-a-dozen railway routes in the north of England are facing a similar threat. The problem is a worn out system and an almost total lack of cash to repair it. Bridges and tunnels are showing their age, the wooden supports for the tracks are rotting and engines and coaches are getting old.

On major lines between large cities, the problem is not too bad. These lines still make a profit and cash can be found to maintain them. But on the country branch line, the story is different. As track wears out, it is not replaced. Instead speed limits are introduced, making journeys longer than necessary and discouraging customers.

If a bridge is dangerous, there is often only one thing for British Rail to do: go out and find money from another source. This is exactly what it did a few months ago when a bridge at Bridlington station was threatening to fall down. Repairs were estimated at £200,000 – just for one bridge – and British Rail was delighted, and rather surprised, when two local councils offered half that amount between them.

26  Since 1970 Dent Station has been used
    A  only for a part of each year.
    B  only in some years.
    C  only by local people.
    D  only by hill walkers.

27  Of all the railway routes in Britain the one which passes through Dent
    A  is the most historic.
    B  passes through the most attractive countryside.
    C  is the most expensive to maintain.
    D  carries the greatest number of tourists.

28  The most urgent problem for many country railway lines is that of
    A  rebuilding bridges.
    B  repairing engines.
    C  renewing coaches.
    D  repairing stations.

29  The people most affected by the difficulties facing British Rail would appear to be
    A  business men.
    B  organised groups of holiday makers.
    C  inter-city travellers.
    D  occasional and local travellers.

30  In order to improve the financial situation of country railway lines British Rail should
    A  introduce speed limits.
    B  reduce the scale of maintenance.
    C  increase fares.
    D  appeal to local councils.

31  The prospect the country railway lines might close is viewed by the author with
    A  anger.
    B  approval.
    C  regret.
    D  surprise.

## SECOND PASSAGE

In the primary school, a child is in a comparatively simple setting and most of the time forms a relationship with one familiar teacher. On entering secondary school, a new world opens up and frequently it is a much more difficult world. The pupil soon learns to be less free in the way he speaks to teachers and even to his fellow pupils. He begins to lose gradually the free and easy ways of the primary school, for he senses the need for a more cautious approach in the secondary school where there are older pupils. Secondary staff and pupils suffer from the pressures of academic work and seem to have less time to stop and talk. Teachers with specialist roles may see hundreds of children in a week, and a pupil may be able to form relationships with very few of the staff. He has to decide which adults are approachable; good schools will make clear to every young person from the first year what guidance and personal help is available – but whether the reality of life in the institution actually encourages requests for help is another matter.

Adults often forget what a confusing picture school can offer to a child. He sees a great deal of movement, a great number of people – often rather frightening-looking people – and realises that an increasing number of choices and decisions have to be made. As he progresses through the school the confusion may become less but the choices and decisions required will increase. The school will rightly expect the pupil to take the first steps to obtain the help he needs, for this is the pattern of adult life for which he has to be prepared, but all the time the opportunities for personal and group advice must be presented in a way which makes them easy to understand and within easy reach of pupils.

32  According to the passage one of the problems for pupils entering secondary schools is that
   A  they are taught by many different teachers.
   B  they do not attend lessons in every subject.
   C  the teachers do not want to be friendly.
   D  the teachers give most attention to the more academic pupils.

33  In secondary schools every pupil having problems should
   A  know how to ask for help.
   B  be freed from any pressure of academic work.
   C  be able to discuss his problems in class.
   D  be able to discuss his problems with any teacher.

34  In this passage about secondary schools, the author is mainly concerned about
   A  academic standards.
   B  the role of specialist teachers.
   C  the training of the individual teachers.
   D  the personal development of pupils.

THIRD PASSAGE

# Dulux Colours in a Full Range of Finishes –
# The Best Paint for the Job

**FOR WALLS AND CEILINGS —**
*Dulux Vinyl Matt* – With ICI Vinyl for a washable, matt finish on interior walls and ceilings, 1 litre is sufficient for approximately 12 sq metres (14 sq yards).

*Dulux Vinyl Silk* – With ICI Vinyl for a washable, smooth silk finish on interior walls and ceilings. Ideal on patterned wallpapers. 1 litre is sufficient for approximately 11 sq metres (13 sq yards).

**FOR WOODWORK AND METAL —**
*Dulux Primers* – A range of Primers which must be used before any undercoating or painting on bare wood, metal and plaster surfaces. For further information, see "Dulux Successful Painting And You".

*Dulux Undercoat* – Forms the perfect surface for Dulux Gloss Finish. For wood and metal, inside and out, 1 litre is sufficient for approximately 15 sq metres (18 sq yards).

*Dulux Gloss Finish* – With ICI Silthane, harder-wearing than Polyurethane alone. Tough high-gloss finish. For wood and metal, inside and out. For the best results, use Dulux Undercoat. 1 litre is sufficient for approximately 17 sq metres (20 sq yards).

*Dulux Non-Drip Gloss* – With ICI Silthane, harder-wearing than Polyurethane alone. A different kind of Non-Drip Gloss. More manageable, goes on easier for a better, smoother high-gloss finish. For wood and metal, inside and out. 1 litre is sufficient for approximately 12 sq metres (14 sq yards).

**FOR EXTERNAL WALLS —**
*Dulux Weathershield* – The smooth paint for external stone walls. In a full range of Town and Country Colours. See the special Weathershield Colour Card. 1 litre is sufficient for approximately 4–10 sq metres (5–12 sq yards). (Spreading rate varies considerably, depending on the roughness of the surface.)

**FOR ALL SURFACES —**
*Dulux Silthane Silk* – An oil-based silk, ideal when a particularly tough, resistant finish is required on interior walls and ceilings. A most beautiful smooth silk finish. For interior woodwork and metal, 1 litre is sufficient for approximately 12 sq metres (14 sq yards).

**FOR A RANGE OF COLOURS —**
*Dulux Matchmaker* – For an even wider choice of fashion colours, see our Matchmaker Colour Cards. 432 colours mixed for your individual colour requirements, available in gloss, matt and silk finishes.

If you would like further information about our Colour Scheming Service and our free guide to successful painting, ask your stockist or contact Retail Customer Services Section, Decorative Paints Dept, ICI Paints Division, Wexham Road, Slough SL2 5DS. Telephone Slough 31151.

35  A tin of Dulux Vinyl Matt compared to a tin of Dulux Vinyl Silk
    A   is more suitable for ceilings.
    B   is less suitable for ceilings.
    C   covers a larger area.
    D   covers a smaller area.

36  For woodwork and metal, how many kinds of paint should be used to get the best results?
    A   1
    B   2
    C   3
    D   4

37  You have two small boys who enjoy a lot of rough play. What would be your best choice of paint for the walls of their playroom?
    A   Vinyl Matt
    B   Vinyl Silk
    C   Silthane Silk
    D   Weathershield

38  If you want to paint your walls exactly the same colour as your old carpet, you should consider using
    A   Dulux Vinyl Matt.
    B   Dulux Vinyl Silk.
    C   Dulux Matchmaker.
    D   Dulux Silthane Silk.

39  If you need some advice on painting techniques, what are you recommended to do?
    A   ask a professional painter
    B   ask your neighbours for help
    C   write to the manufacturers
    D   phone for a dealer to call

40  For each kind of paint the advertisement tells you
    A   on which part of the house it should be used.
    B   with which kind of brush it should be used.
    C   how to prepare the paint.
    D   how long it would take to dry.

# PAPER 2  COMPOSITION  (1½ hours)

*Write two only of the following composition exercises. Your answers must follow exactly the instructions given and must be of between 120 and 180 words each.*

1   You are planning to go on holiday to another country next year. Write a letter to a friend inviting him or her to go on the holiday with you, and giving some information about your plans.

2   Some things have been stolen from your house. You go to the police station and tell them all about the burglary, describing the stolen items.

3   Describe a place of great importance in the history of your country.

4   Friends or family: which do you think have played the more important part in your life?

5   Based on your reading of any one of these books, write on *one* of the following.

   JANE AUSTEN: *Sense and Sensibility*
   What do you think of Willoughby's behaviour?

   G. B. SHAW: *Arms and the Man*
   At the beginning of the play, Raina is engaged to Sergius, and Louka to Nicola. Explain how these engagements are broken and both girls acquire new fiancés.

   GRAHAM GREENE: *The Third Man*
   Towards the end of the story, Colonel Calloway sets a trap for Harry Lime. Describe the trap and its consequences.

## PAPER 3   USE OF ENGLISH   (2 hours)

1  *Fill each of the numbered blanks in the following passage. Use only **one** word in each space.*

In my childhood, the whole family would sometimes go on a diet. ............(1) that we were all oversize; far from ............(2). In fact, one of my brothers was and ............(3) is one of the thinnest people I have ............(4) known. The ............(5) for all this dieting was partly my father's health and ............(6) my mother's strange ideas. My father had heart trouble ............(7) quite some time and the doctor advised him to cut ............(8) on fats and smoking. My mother ............(9) this as a sign that all of us should restrain ............(10) from overeating and she immediately cut our food portions ............(11) half. My brothers and I were ............(12) hungry that we ............(13) to spend our pocket money ............(14) cream cakes. We ............(15) not have worried though. After only a week we surprised our mother secretly ............(16) a slice of fruit cake in the kitchen. We teased her ............(17) this, and my father said life wasn't ............(18) living unless you ............(19) eat whatever you wanted. So she agreed ............(20) start cooking more.

[68]

2  Finish each of the following sentences in such a way that it means exactly the same as the sentence printed before it.

   EXAMPLE: I haven't enjoyed myself so much for years.

   ANSWER: It's years *since I enjoyed myself so much.*

   a) John only understood very little of what the teacher said.

      John could hardly ........................................................

   b) Unless someone has a key, we can't get into the house.

      We can only get ........................................................

   c) I'm sure you didn't lock the front door. Here's the key.

      You can't ........................................................

   d) He prefers golf to tennis.

      He'd rather ........................................................

   e) He is sorry now that he didn't invite Molly to his party.

      He wishes ........................................................

   f) 'Bring your swimming things in case it's sunny.'

      He told ........................................................

   g) There's no need for you to talk so loudly.

      You don't ........................................................

   h) I haven't been to Bristol for three years.

      The last time ........................................................

   i) No one has signed this cheque.

      This cheque ........................................................

   j) Tim will be eighteen next week.

      It's Tim's ........................................................

Practice Test 4

3  Complete the following sentences with the correct form of **forget, remember** or **remind**.

EXAMPLE: I have always *remembered* what happened on that day.

a) I shall never ................................ that wonderful holiday in Italy.

b) When she got old she couldn't ................................ which day of the week it was.

c) Your friend ................................ me of my Uncle in Holland.

d) It's easier to study history if you can ................................ facts easily.

e) Look at all the lights on in the main building. It look as if the caretaker has ................................ to turn them off.


4  The word in capitals at the end of each of the following sentences can be used to form a word that fits suitably in the blank space. Fill each blank in this way.

EXAMPLE: He said 'Good morning' in a most *friendly* way.   FRIEND

a) Craig's old jacket was so ................................ that he had to buy a new one.
   WEAR

b) The ring was not valuable; in fact it was almost ................................
   WORTH

c) During his speech, he kept on ................................ his tie.
   STRAIGHT

d) The water in this area is ................................ and should not be drunk.
   PURE

e) A successful business needs good ................................ .
   ORGANISE

f) Alison's ................................ made it hard for her to speak in public.
   SHY

5  *The Director of a firm is interviewing Henry Jenkins for the Sales Manager's job in his Company. Fill in the parts of the dialogue, numbered (1) to (5), which have been left blank.*

Director: Come in Mr. Jenkins, do sit down. (1) Did ................................................
................................................................................................................?

Henry: Yes, thank you, the traffic isn't too heavy at this time of day.

Director: Why (2) ................................................................................................?

Henry: I want to work for a big company like yours with its extensive international trade, instead of the small company I work for now.

Director: Does (3) ................................................................................................?

Henry: No, not at all. That's why I want to leave, to gain experience of exporting.

Director: Could (4) ................................................................................................?

Henry: I hope so. In my present job I organise a sales team of ten.

Director: When (5) ................................................................................................?

Henry: My present contract lasts until the end of the month.

[71]

6  Write in the spaces indicated, using about 80 words for each, what the people might say when asked to describe in turn the advantages and disadvantages of their particular job from the point of view of

        money                  chances of promotion

        hours of work        contact with people

*As a bank clerk*

*I'm a nurse, and things are quite different for me*

# PAPER 4   LISTENING COMPREHENSION
(about 30 minutes)

## FIRST PART

1   The catering manager of a hotel is talking to his secretary on the phone. He is telling her what she has to order for the kitchen today. Complete the order form which she is filling in as she talks. Some of the information has already been filled in for you.

---

**GRAND HOTELS PLC**

MARINE AVENUE
SUNBURY ON SEA

Date: 17/8/86

KITCHEN ORDER FORM

To (Supplier):

| Standard items | Quantity | Notes |
|---|---|---|
| Apples | 15 kilos | English if possible |
| Cabbage | | white |
| Lemons | 2 cases | |
| Onions | 20 kilos | |
| Peas | | not too good |
| Peppers | | |
| Potatoes | | ordinary |
| Tomatoes | | |

| Special items | Quantity |
|---|---|
| 1  White seedless grapes | 6 kilos |
| 2 | |

Practice Test 4

## SECOND PART

*For questions 2–6 tick (✓) one of the boxes A, B, C or D.*

2   The date of the meeting has to be changed because
    A   Graham is ill in bed.
    B   two people cannot come to it.
    C   Maureen Wills has to go somewhere else.
    D   they have been unable to contact Rosemary.

3   Jerry cannot attend the meeting tomorrow evening because he will be
    A   at the dentist's.
    B   at work.
    C   unwell.
    D   too busy.

4   Why can't the new meeting be on Thursday?
    A   Graham has no car that evening.
    B   Graham has to look after the children.
    C   Maureen has to look after the children.
    D   It's Maureen's wedding anniversary.

5   The original problem with meeting on Tuesday is that
    A   Jerry has other plans.
    B   Rosemary cannot come.
    C   Graham's wife needs the car.
    D   Maureen thinks it's too late.

6   The meeting is finally arranged for 7.30 at
    A   Maureen's house on Thursday.
    B   Graham's house on Thursday.
    C   Maureen's house on Tuesday.
    D   Graham's house on Tuesday.

[75]

*Practice Test 4*

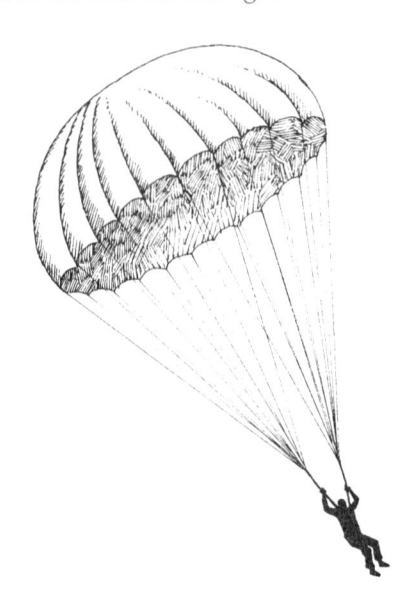

## THIRD PART

*For questions 7–9 tick (✓) one of the boxes A, B, C or D.*

7   Nowadays free fall parachuting is

    A   the most popular sport in Britain.

    B   too expensive for most people.

    C   as popular as cycling.

    D   as popular as ski-jumping.

| A | |
|---|---|
| B | |
| C | |
| D | |

8   Sally Small wanted to write an article about

    A   unusual sports.

    B   things women could do.

    C   being a journalist.

    D   dangerous sports.

| A | |
|---|---|
| B | |
| C | |
| D | |

9   In 'free fall' you

    A   open your parachute at once.

    B   have little control over your movements.

    C   reach speeds of at least 200 m.p.h.

    D   are able to move to left and right.

| A | |
|---|---|
| B | |
| C | |
| D | |

*Practice Test 4*

# PAPER 5  INTERVIEW  (about 15 minutes)

You will be asked to take part in a conversation with a group of other students or with your teacher. The conversation will be based on one particular topic area or theme, for example holidays, work, food.

Of course each interview will be different for each student or group of students, but a *typical* interview is described below.

* At the start of the interview you will be asked to talk about one of the photographs among the Interview Exercises at the back of the book.

* You will then be asked to discuss one of the passages at the back of the book. Your teacher may ask you to talk about its content, where you think it comes from, who the author or speaker is, whether you agree or disagree with it, and so on. You will *not* be asked to read the passage aloud, but you may quote parts of it to make your point.

* You may then be asked to discuss for example an advertisement, a leaflet, extract from a newspaper etc. Your teacher will tell you which of the Interview Exercises to look at.

* You may also be asked to take part in an activity with a group of other students or your teacher. Your teacher will tell you which section among the Interview Exercises you should look at.

# Practice Test 5

## PAPER 1   READING COMPREHENSION   (1 hour)

*Answer all questions. Indicate your choice of answer in every case* **on the separate answer sheet** *already given out, which should show your name and examination index number. Follow carefully the instructions about how to record your answers. Give* **one answer only** *to each question. Marks will not be deducted for wrong answers: your total score on this test will be the number of correct answers you give.*

### SECTION A

*In this section you must choose the word or phrase which best completes each sentence.* **On your answer sheet** *indicate the letter A, B, C or D against the number of each item 1 to 25 for the word or phrase you choose.*

1   From the hotel there is a good .................... of the mountains.
    A  vision     B  view     C  sight     D  picture

2   I'm sorry, I haven't got ....................change. Why don't you try the bank?
    A  some     B  lots     C  any     D  all

3   If it .................... fine, I shall go out.
    A  was     B  is     C  were     D  will be

4   We've .................... of time to catch the train so there's no need to rush.
    A  very much     B  enough     C  great deal     D  plenty

5   I can't make .................... what's happening.
    A  away     B  out     C  do     D  over

6   He's left his book at home; he's always so ....................
    A  forgetting     B  forgotten     C  forgettable     D  forgetful

7   Driving a car with faulty brakes is .................... quite a risk.
    A  putting     B  setting     C  taking     D  being

8   If we had known your new address, we .................... to see you.
    A  came     B  will come     C  would come     D  would have come

9  A small .......... of students was waiting outside the class to see the teacher.
   A gang    B crowd    C team    D group

10 Jenny and her sister are so .........., they could almost be twins.
   A likeness    B alike    C same    D the same

11 He went to Australia hoping to find a teaching .......... without too much difficulty.
   A work    B occupation    C employment    D post

12 We'll play tennis and .......... we'll have lunch.
   A then    B straight away    C immediately    D so

13 I hope he's .......... to buy some bread; there's hardly any left.
   A reminded    B proposed    C suggested    D remembered

14 The accused man .......... to give the police any more information.
   A objected    B denied    C refused    D disliked

15 Take the number 7 bus and get .......... at Forest Road.
   A up    B down    C outside    D off

16 There is no .......... in going to school if you're not willing to learn.
   A reason    B aim    C point    D purpose

17 She complained .......... when she heard that she had to work on Sunday.
   A severely    B bitterly    C extremely    D terribly

18 For a long time after the accident, he suffered from constant .......... in his back.
   A hurt    B ache    C pain    D injury

19 The policeman .......... me the way.
   A told    B said    C explained    D directed

20 It was a very beautiful cloth .......... from silk.
   A composed    B worn    C woven    D threaded

21 My mother was .......... of making a cake when the front door bell rang.
   A at the centre    B on her way    C in the middle    D halfway through

22 .......... you do better work than this, you won't pass the exam.
   A Although    B If    C Unless    D When

23 If you want to join the History Society, you must first .......... this application form.
   A make up    B write down    C fill in    D do up

24  He has just taken an examination .................. chemistry.
    A  on      B  about      C  for      D  in

25  The police have asked that .................. who saw the accident should get in touch with them.
    A  somebody    B  someone    C  one    D  anyone

### SECTION B

*In this section you will find after each of the passages a number of questions or unfinished statements about the passage, each with four suggested answers or ways of finishing. You must choose the one which you think fits best.* **On your answer sheet** *indicate the letter A, B, C or D against the number of each item 26–40 for the answer you choose. Give one answer only to each question. Read each passage right through before choosing your answers.*

FIRST PASSAGE

By far the most common snake in Britain is the adder. In Scotland, in fact, there are no other snakes at all. The adder is also the only British snake with a poisonous bite. It can be found almost anywhere, but prefers sunny hillsides and rough open country, including high ground. In Ireland there are no snakes at all.

Most people regard snake bites as a fatal misfortune, but not all bites are serious, and very few are fatal. Sometimes attempts at emergency treatment turn out to be more dangerous than the bite itself, with amateurs heroically, but mistakenly, trying do-it-yourself surgery and other unnecessary measures.

All snakes have small teeth, so it follows that all snakes can bite, but only the bite of the adder presents any danger. British snakes are shy animals and are far more frightened of you than you could possibly be of them. The adder will attack only if it feels threatened, as can happen if you take it by surprise and step on it accidentally, or if you try to catch it or pick it up, which it dislikes intensely. If it hears you coming, it will normally get out of the way as quickly as it can, but adders cannot move very rapidly and may attack before moving if you are very close.

The effect of a bite varies considerably. It depends upon several things, one of which is the body-weight of the person bitten. The bigger the person, the less harmful the bite is likely to be, which is why children suffer far more seriously from snake bites than adults. A healthy person will also have better resistance against the poison.

Very few people actually die from snake bites in Britain, and though these bites can make some people very ill, there are probably just as many cases of bites having little or no effect, as there are of serious illness.

[80]

26  Adders are most likely to be found
    A  in wilder parts of Britain and Ireland.
    B  in Scotland and nowhere else.
    C  on uncultivated land throughout Britain.
    D  in shady fields in England.

27  If you are with someone who is bitten by an adder you should
    A  try to catch the adder.
    B  make no attempt to treat the bite.
    C  not worry about the victim.
    D  operate as soon as possible.

28  We are told that adders are
    A  normally friendly towards people.
    B  unlikely to bite except in self-defence.
    C  aggressive towards anyone in their territory.
    D  not afraid of human beings.

29  If an adder hears you approaching, it will usually
    A  move out of your path.
    B  take no notice of you at all.
    C  disappear very quickly.
    D  wait until you are close then attack.

30  We are told that in general British people think snakes are
    A  not very common in Britain.
    B  usually harmless.
    C  more dangerous than they usually are.
    D  unlikely to kill people by their bite.

SECOND PASSAGE

An industrial society, especially one as centralised and concentrated as that of Britain, is heavily dependent on certain essential services: for instance, electricity supply, water, rail and road transport, the harbours. The area of dependency has widened to include removing rubbish, hospital and ambulance services, and, as the economy develops, central computer and information services as well. If any of these services ceases to operate, the whole economic system is in danger.

It is this interdependency of the economic system which makes the power of trade unions such an important issue. Single trade unions have the ability to cut off many countries' economic blood supply. This can happen more easily in Britain than in some other countries, in part because the labour force is highly organised. About 55 per cent of British workers belong to unions, compared to under a quarter in the United States.

*Practice Test 5*

For historical reasons, Britain's unions have tended to develop along trade and occupational lines, rather than on an industry-by-industry basis, which makes a wages policy, democracy in industry and the improvement of procedures for fixing wage levels difficult to achieve.

There are considerable strains and tensions in the trade union movement, some of them arising from their outdated and inefficient structure. Some unions have lost many members because of industrial changes. Others are involved in arguments about who should represent workers in new trades. Unions for skilled trades are separate from general unions, which means that different levels of wages for certain jobs are often a source of bad feeling between unions. In traditional trades which are being pushed out of existence by advancing technologies, unions can fight for their members' disappearing jobs to the point where the jobs of other unions' members are threatened or destroyed. The printing of newspapers both in the United States and in Britain has frequently been halted by the efforts of printers to hold on to their traditional highly-paid jobs.

Trade unions have problems of internal communication just as managers in companies do, problems which multiply in very large unions or in those which bring workers in very different industries together into a single general union. Some trade union officials have to be re-elected regularly; others are elected, or even appointed, for life. Trade union officials have to work with a system of 'shop stewards' in many unions, 'shop stewards' being workers elected by other workers as their representatives at factory or works level.

31 Why is the question of trade union power important in Britain?
   A The economy is very interdependent.
   B Unions have been established a long time.
   C There are more unions in Britain than elsewhere.
   D There are many essential services.

32 Why is it difficult to improve the procedures for fixing wage levels?
   A Some industries have no unions.
   B Unions are not organised according to industries.
   C Only 55 per cent of workers belong to unions.
   D Some unions are too powerful.

33 Because of their out-of-date organisation some unions find it difficult to
   A change as industries change.
   B get new members to join.
   C learn new technologies.
   D bargain for high enough wages.

34 Disagreements arise between unions because some of them
   A try to win over members of other unions.
   B ignore agreements.
   C protect their own members at the expense of others.
   D take over other union's jobs.

35 In what ways are unions and large companies similar?
  A  Both have too many managers.
  B  Both have problems in passing on information.
  C  Both lose touch with individual workers.
  D  Both their managements are too powerful.

36 What basic problem are we told most trade unions face?
  A  They are not equal in size or influence.
  B  They are not organised efficiently.
  C  They are less powerful than employers' organisations.
  D  They do not have enough members.

Practice Test 5

THIRD PASSAGE

# *Breakaways*
### Short break holidays throughout Britain

# Win A Super Value Breakaway Weekend For 2

This is your chance to win a Breakaway weekend for two people at any of the 83 Breakaway hotels throughout Britain.

To win the Breakaway weekend for two, answer these four questions and send your entry, to arrive not later than 31 July 1985, to Team House, 24 Church Street, Ashford, Kent. TN25 5BJ.

> 1. The St Vincent Rocks Hotel, Bristol is on the edge of the Avon Gorge which is crossed by the Clifton Bridge. Who designed the bridge?
>
> 2. The Aerodrome Hotel, Croydon is next to the airfield from which England's famous solo pilot made her record flights in the 1930s. Who was she?
>
> 3. The Talbot Hotel, Oundle, Northants is not far from the village of Fotheringay and the castle where one of history's most famous queens was imprisoned. Who was she?
>
> 4. The Larkfield Hotel, Maidstone is a few miles away from one of England's top motor racing tracks. What is the name of the track?

The person whose correct entry is picked out first by a computer will win the prize. This decision is final. The winner will be sent a super value Breakaway booklet giving details of the 83 hotels from which he/she can choose where to spend the prize weekend.

Every Breakaway hotel gives you the chance to see something different, while providing you with comfortable surroundings and good food.

A Breakaway weekend includes a three-course dinner, accommodation and a full English breakfast, for two nights. You also get Sunday lunch, either a traditional meal at your hotel, or, if you are planning to go sightseeing, the hotel will provide a packed lunch for you.

Breakaway hotels are great places for families. Children can choose from their own special menu, and for those up to 12 years old accommodation is free of charge when sharing a room with their parents.

A super value Breakaway booklet will be sent to you if you contact this number: 0252 517517.

37  This competition will be won by the person
    A  who sends in the first correct answers.
    B  whose correct entry is selected by a computer.
    C  whose entry arrives first on 31 July.
    D  whose entry is the final one selected by the computer.

38  Question 4 in the competition is different from the others because
    A  the hotel described is a modern one.
    B  it asks about a place not a person.
    C  the hotel can be reached easily by car.
    D  the answer is the name of a man.

39  The winner's weekend will include
    A  a free room for children under 12.
    B  dinner on two days and one lunch.
    C  dinner and packed lunches on two days.
    D  light breakfasts in his/her room.

40  The advertisement suggests that the best way to get a Breakaway booklet is to
    A  enter the competition.
    B  write to one of the hotels.
    C  write to Team House.
    D  telephone 0252 517517.

*Practice Test 5*

## PAPER 2   COMPOSITION   (1½ hours)

*Write **two only** of the following composition exercises. Your answers must follow exactly the instructions given and must be of between 120 and 180 words each.*

1.  You have received an invitation to a friend's wedding, but it is impossible for you to accept it. Write a letter to your friend explaining this, and mentioning the present you are sending.

2.  You have a job as a tourist guide, and you have to talk to groups of people about places or buildings in your city. Tell them about one particularly interesting place to visit.

3.  'Thank God it was only a dream!' Write a story ending with these words.

4.  Computers and other machines are becoming more and more important in everyday life. Do you welcome this trend, or dislike it?

5.  Based on your reading of any one of these books, write on *one* of the following.

    G. B. SHAW: *Arms and the Man*
    'The soul of a servant'. Explain how this phrase is used in the play.

    *Outstanding Short Stories* (LONGMAN)
    Tell the story of Susan Bell as if you were Aaron Dunn *or* Kate O'Brien.

    PETER DICKINSON: *The Seventh Raven*
    Describe the 'opera mafia' and explain why it has this name.

## PAPER 3   USE OF ENGLISH   (2 hours)

1  *Fill each of the numbered blanks in the following passage. Use only **one** word in each space.*

I used to go into the countryside to sketch animals and plants, carrying my drawing materials in a bag. One day I was walking across a field, looking ................ (1) rabbits to draw. Lost ................ (2) thought, I ................ (3) not noticed a bull running towards me. About one hundred metres ................ (4) was a tree under ................ (5) I intended to sit and draw. Suddenly, I ................ (6) a noise behind me. I turned and saw the bull. I knew that a bull can run ................ (7) faster ................ (8) a man, but I also knew that a bull cannot see very ................ (9) and notices only shape and movement. I ................ (10) not panic but ran towards the tree, keeping the ................ (11), myself and the bull in a straight line. To distract the bull, I then threw my bag to the right, so it was out of the line of the tree. The bull saw ................ (12) sudden movement and headed towards the bag. I ................ (13) the tree and climbed up it. From ................ (14) I watched the bull attacking my bag with its horns and feet. It continued to ................ (15) this for fifteen minutes and I was very ................ (16) to be up the tree. ................ (17), the bull was satisfied and moved off. I waited until it was a very long way ................ (18) and then got down from the tree and picked up my bag. I left the field as fast as I ................ (19) and then looked inside my bag. Everything in it was ................ (20) ruined.

[87]

Practice Test 5

2  Finish each of the following sentences in such a way that it means exactly the same as the sentence printed before it.

EXAMPLE: I haven't enjoyed myself so much for years.

ANSWER: It's years *since I enjoyed myself so much.*

a) Unless he phones immediately he won't get any information.

If he doesn't phone immediately, he won't get any information.

b) How long is it since they bought the house?

When did they buy the house?

c) He couldn't repair the broken vase.

The broken vase can not be repaired.

d) The garden still needs digging.

The garden hasn't been dug enough.

e) Have you got a cheaper carpet than this?

Is this the cheapest carpet you have got?

f) I can't get my feet into these shoes.

These shoes are too small for me to wear them.

g) I am very pleased that we shall meet again soon.

I am looking forward to meet you again soon.

h) 'Keep away from this area,' said the security guard, when we approached the fence.

The security guard told me to keep away from this area when we approach the fence.

i) I've never met such a famous person before.

It's the first time a met a person so famous.

j) This pudding can be cooked in its tin.

You don't need to cook this pudding out its tin.

[88]

Practice Test 5

3 Complete the following sentences by writing in the space provided a suitable word meaning the opposite of the word in capital letters.

EXAMPLE: Cinderella was very BEAUTIFUL, but both her sisters were very *ugly*.

a) Although the earlier scientific experiments had been FAILURES this one was a complete ...*success*...

b) The first eight battles fought by the General resulted in his DEFEAT, so his final ............................ surprised everyone.

c) He was not sure if turning the screw to the left would TIGHTEN it or ................................ it.

d) Make sure the bread you buy is ...*fresh*... not STALE.

e) The water in the tank always FREEZES at night but the ice soon ...*melts*... when the sun comes up.

4 Complete the following sentences with an expression formed from **put**.

EXAMPLE: You must *put out* the lights before you leave.

a) That man is so rude I just can't ...*put*... ...*up*... ...*with*... his behaviour any longer.

b) Because she kept ...*putting*... ...*on*... going to the dentist, her toothache got worse.

c) You are ...*put*... ...*on*... weight. You'll have to stop eating chocolate.

d) Look at this mess! ...*out*... your toys ...*away*... at once.

[89]

*Practice Test 5*

5  Complete the following dialogue.

(In the Tourist Information Office, Avebury, Wiltshire, England.)

Tourist:  Are there any interesting walks we can take in the countryside in this area?

Officer:  Oh yes, there's the 'Ridgeway Path'. It's a very popular place to walk.

Tourist:  (1) ............................................................................................................. ?

Officer:  150 kilometres. It's one of our long-distance footpaths.

Tourist:  (2) ............................................................................................................. !

Officer:  Oh, you don't have to walk all of it. You can do just a part.

Tourist:  (3) ............................................................................................................. ?

Officer:  No, ordinary shoes will do, at this time of year anyway. Of course, you shouldn't wear high-heels or anything like that.

Tourist:  (4) ............................................................................................................. ?

Officer:  No, I'm sure that won't happen. The path is easy to follow and there are plenty of signs.

Tourist:  (5) ............................................................................................................. ?

Officer:  Lots of interesting historical and archaeological sites, and some marvellous views from the hills. We believe the path is over 5,000 years old. We have a map and a guide-book which explain all about it.

Tourist:  (6) ............................................................................................................. ?

Officer:  The map is 80p and the guide-book is £1.50p.

Tourist:  (7) .............................................................................................................

Officer:  Here you are. That will be £2.30p, please.

6 Study the illustration showing the cost and journey time of different ways of travelling from London to Manchester, and the notes below. Complete the paragraphs on page 92 in the spaces provided, explaining which way you think each person should travel in winter when the weather is bad. (You may choose any way for any person, provided you give reasons.)

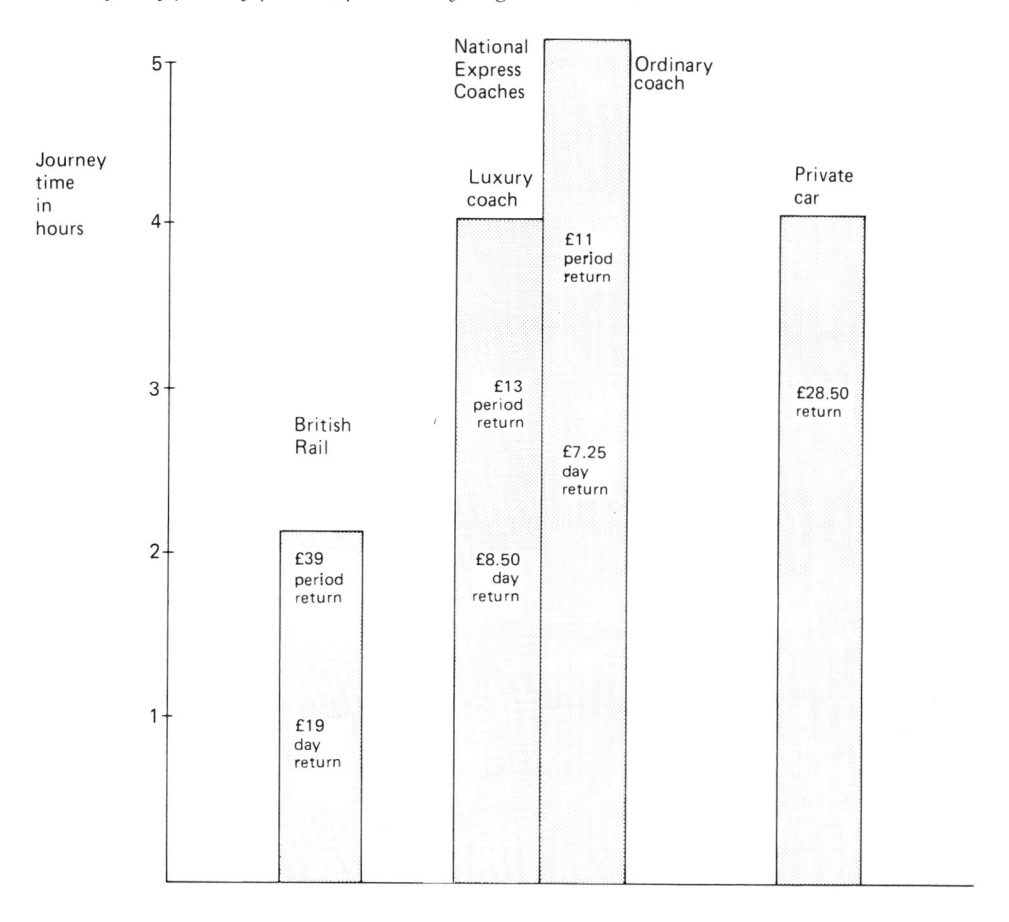

London – Manchester: journey times and fares.

Notes

1. Day return ticket – you must go and come back the same day.

2. Period return ticket – you can go and come back up to three months later.

3. Luxury coaches have reclining seats, toilets, food and drink, hostesses, and video films. Ordinary coaches have none of these.

4. The cost of the car journey includes all the costs of running a car, not just petrol costs.

5. Students and children can get reductions on trains but not on coaches.

Practice Test 5

Philip Smith    aged 23. He needs to go to Manchester, where he has never been before, for an interview for a new job and must be there by 10 a.m. All his expenses will be paid by the the company. He has a car.

I think Philip Smith will go by ................................... (Cost £           )

because ............................................................................................................

............................................................................................................

............................................................................................................

............................................................................................................

Agnes Clark    aged 72. She needs to go to Manchester to look after her sister who has just left hospital. If Agnes sits down for long periods of time, she gets terrible pains in her legs.

In my opinion Agnes Clark will go by ................... (Cost £           )

because ............................................................................................................

............................................................................................................

............................................................................................................

............................................................................................................

James Norris    aged 42. He is going to Manchester with his wife and two children to spend the Christmas holiday, as usual, with his parents. He has a car.

It would be best for James to travel by ................... (Cost £           )

because ............................................................................................................

............................................................................................................

............................................................................................................

............................................................................................................

Mary Stevens    aged 22. She is going to Manchester to spend the weekend with her boyfriend and his family. She was a student at London University and has just started her first job. She hasn't got a car.

I believe Mary Stevens will choose to go by ................... (Cost £           )

because ............................................................................................................

............................................................................................................

............................................................................................................

............................................................................................................

[92]

Practice Test 5

# PAPER 4 LISTENING COMPREHENSION
(about 30 minutes)

### FIRST PART

*For questions 1–4 tick (✓) one of the boxes A, B, C or D.*

1  Lona spent her childhood
   A  in North Carolina.
   B  on a dairy farm.
   C  in Florida.
   D  on the West Coast.

2  Lona likes reading about
   A  sewing.
   B  science fiction.
   C  history.
   D  travel.

3  Lona and her family have
   A  spent holidays in Austria.
   B  been on trips to Virginia.
   C  spent holidays in the U.K.
   D  been on trips to the West Coast.

4  Living where she does Lona misses
   A  winter sports.
   B  seasonal changes.
   C  snow and ice.
   D  water sports.

[93]

Practice Test 5

## SECOND PART

*Listen to the conversation between the old lady and her neighbour, and then fill in the spaces in this note. Be as brief as possible.*

---

What to do while the old lady is away!

5. She'll be back on _____.

6. Tins of cat food _____ the fridge.

7. Give the cat _____ tin(s) each day.

8. Water the garden if _____.

9. Water the tomatoes _____.

10. Water the houseplants _____.

11. Leave the _____ on sometimes.

12. Her phone number while she's away will be _____.

Practice Test 5

## THIRD PART

*For questions 13–20 tick (✓) whether the statements are true or false.*

|    |                                                                          | True | False |
|----|--------------------------------------------------------------------------|------|-------|
| 13 | Suggestions are given on what to do both in and around the city.         |      |       |
| 14 | The zoo is open every day of the year.                                   |      |       |
| 15 | Buses take 50 minutes to reach the zoo.                                  |      |       |
| 16 | A dancing display will take place at the Ross Open Air Theatre.          |      |       |
| 17 | Refreshments are available in Duddingston Church in the afternoon.       |      |       |
| 18 | Coach tours of the city start from St Andrew's Square.                   |      |       |
| 19 | The Camera Obscura should be visited at night.                           |      |       |
| 20 | An orchestral concert will take place in the King's Theatre this evening.|      |       |

[95]

Practice Test 5

## FOURTH PART

*Listen to this conversation between two people who work in a hospital and have to provide equipment for the nurses' training programme; fill in the details in the diary.*

*Fill in the gaps 21–23 on the page from the diary shown below.*

---

29 Thursday
　　　　　　　　　　　　　　　　Health Centre
　　　　　　　　　　　　　　in Lecture Theatre
　　　　　　　　　　　　　　　requires TV

30 Friday
　　　　㉑ ................. Foundation
　　　　㉒ in .................
　　　　㉓ requires projector and ..................

1 Saturday
　　　　　　　　　　　　　　　In-service training
　　　　　　　　　　　　　　in Lecture Theatre
　　　　　　　　　　　　　requires mic + speakers

[96]

## PAPER 5  INTERVIEW  (about 15 minutes)

You will be asked to take part in a conversation with a group of other students or with your teacher. The conversation will be based on one particular topic area or theme, for example holidays, work, food.

Of course each interview will be different for each student or group of students, but a *typical* interview is described below.

* At the start of the interview you will be asked to talk about one of the photographs among the Interview Exercises at the back of the book.

* You will then be asked to discuss one of the passages at the back of the book. Your teacher may ask you to talk about its content, where you think it comes from, who the author or speaker is, whether you agree or disagree with it, and so on. You will *not* be asked to read the passage aloud, but you may quote parts of it to make your point.

* You may then be asked to discuss for example an advertisement, a leaflet, extract from a newspaper etc. Your teacher will tell you which of the Interview Exercises to look at.

* You may also be asked to take part in an activity with a group of other students or your teacher. Your teacher will tell you which section among the Interview Exercises you should look at.

# Interview Exercises

THE WEATHER

**1**

**2** I'm afraid we are unable to bring you the highlights of today's match, which was cancelled owing to rain. The covers were put over the ground at about 1.30 and the rain has been almost continuous ever since. Both teams are hoping that play can be resumed as quickly as possible.

**3** Autumn did its best to make up for the dreadful summer we had this year by giving some areas their hottest day of the year and the best October weather for 64 years. In Norfolk temperatures rose to 27.9 degrees Celsius, that's 82.2 Fahrenheit.

**4** I remember we once got stuck in the snow on the motorway and we were there for an hour and a half. Fortunately we managed to keep warm but there were cases that winter where people froze to death in their cars. Once you lose your body heat you can be in a very dangerous position.

**5**

## Cool with showers

ALL AREAS will remain under the influence of a slow moving depression centred to the south-west of Ireland.

**London, SE, E Anglia, Cent S England; E Midlands:** Dry and bright at first. Showers developing during the afternoon, merging to give longer periods of rain in the evening. Wind SE, light or moderate. Max temp 13 to 15C (55 to 59F).

**E, NW, Cent N and NE England, Lake District, Isle of Man:** Sunny intervals. Showers developing, some heavy. Wind SE, light or moderate. Max 12 to 14C (54 to 57F).

**W Midlands, Channel Islands, SW England, S and N Wales:** Bright at first. Showers, some heavy, developing widely with some longer periods of rain. Wind SE moderate. Max 12 to 14C (54 to 57F).

**Borders, Edinburgh and Dundee, Aberdeen, SW Scotland, Glasgow, Cent Highlands, Argyll, N Ireland:** Outbreaks of rain, some heavy at first. Sunny intervals developing but also scattered showers. Wind SE, light or moderate. Max 11 to 13C (52 to 55F).

**Moray Firth, NE and NW Scotland, Orkney, Shetland:** Dry at first. Outbreaks of rain spreading from S, clearing later. Wind E or SE, light or moderate. Max 9 to 11C (48 to 52F).

**Outlook:** Continuing unsettled, with showers and sunny intervals.

### AROUND THE WORLD
Lunch–time Reports

|  | C F |  | C F |
|---|---|---|---|
| Ajaccio | R 16 61 | *L. Angeles | S 19 66 |
| Algiers | S 22 72 | Luxembourg | F 18 64 |
| Amsterdam | F 18 64 | Madrid | R 11 52 |
| Athens | F 19 66 | Majorca | S 20 68 |
| Bahrain |  | Malaga | F 21 70 |
| *Barbados | F 29 84 | Malta | S 21 70 |
| Barcelona | F 18 64 | Manchester | R 11 52 |
| Beirut |  | Melbourne | S 14 57 |
| Belgrade | S 22 72 | *Mexico C | S 21 70 |
| Berlin | S 23 73 | *Miami | F 24 75 |
| *Bermuda | F 20 68 | *Montreal | F 8 46 |
| Biarritz | F 15 59 | Moscow | C 5 41 |
| Birmingham | R 8 46 | Munich | S 22 72 |
| Bombay | S 32 90 | Nairobi | F 25 77 |
| Bordeaux | F 14 57 | Naples | F 20 68 |
| *Boston | C 11 52 | *Nassau | F 27 81 |
| Boulogne | C 12 54 | Newcastle | R 8 46 |
| Bristol | C 11 52 | New Delhi | S 36 97 |
| Brussels | S 19 66 | *New York | S 13 55 |
| Budapest | S 22 72 | Nice | C 15 59 |
| *Buenos A | S 23 73 | Oporto | F 13 55 |
| Cairo | S 28 82 | Oslo | F 21 70 |
| Cape Town | S 25 77 | Paris | C 13 55 |
| Cardiff | C 11 52 | Peking | S 28 82 |
| Casablanca | S 18 64 | Perth |  |
| *Chicago | S 21 70 | Prague | S 24 75 |
| Cologne | C 20 68 | Reykjavik | S 5 41 |
| Copenhagen | S 16 61 | Rhodes | S 22 72 |
| Corfu | R 18 64 | *Rio de Jan | S 27 81 |
| Dublin | F 10 50 | Riyadh | S 31 88 |
| Dubrovnik | S 20 68 | Rome |  |
| Edinburgh | R 10 50 | Salzburg | S 26 79 |
| Faro | C 17 63 | Seoul | S 26 79 |
| Florence | S 23 73 | Singapore | Th 27 81 |
| Frankfurt | F 19 66 | Stockholm | S 21 70 |
| Funchal | C 19 66 | Strasbourg | F 20 68 |
| Geneva | S 20 68 | Sydney | R 16 61 |
| Gibraltar | C 18 64 | Tangier | F 19 66 |
| Glasgow | R 11 52 | Tel-Aviv | S 23 73 |
| Helsinki | S 19 66 | Tenerife | F 22 72 |
| Hong Kong | F 27 81 | Tokyo | R 17 63 |
| Innsbruck | F 24 75 | Tunis | F 20 68 |
| Inverness | R 11 52 | Valencia | F 23 73 |
| Istanbul | S 19 66 | *Vancouver | F 11 52 |
| Johnsbrg | C 14 57 | Venice |  |
| Karachi | S 33 91 | Vienna | S 22 72 |
| Larnaca | S 22 72 | Warsaw | S 19 66 |
| Las Palmas | F 20 68 | *Wshington | F 18 64 |
| Lisbon | C 14 57 | Wellington | S 14 57 |
| Locarno | C 13 55 | Zurich | C 16 61 |
| London | R 10 50 |  |  |

C, cloudy; F, fair; R, rain; S, sunny; T, thunder.

*Previous day's readings.

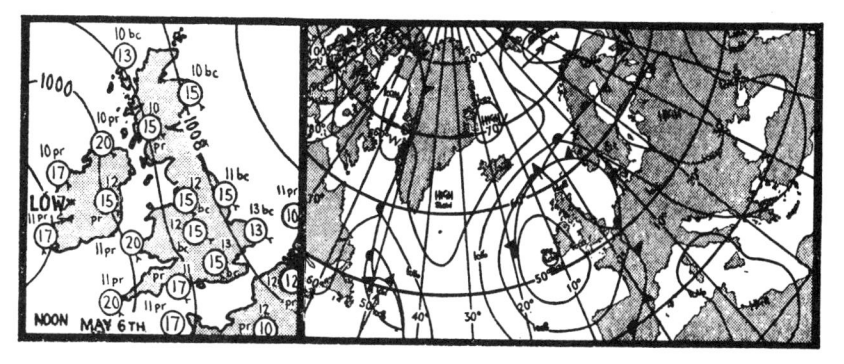

*Interview Exercises*

**6** You live in the North East of England and you would like to go out for the day. Keeping in mind the weather forecast for today on page 99, explain which of the following things you would do. Give reasons for your choice.

    take a boat trip                   visit a ruined castle
    go cycling                        go shopping
    climb a mountain            spend the day at the sea
    visit a museum               see a film

## EATING HABITS

**7**

**8** Clean and scrape the mussels under running water. Throw away any that are already beginning to open. Put them into a large saucepan with a lid and shake them over a brisk heat until they have opened. Allow them to cool a little, then remove the top shells and put a little almond mixture onto each mussel.

*Interview Exercises*

**9** Would you have a few minutes to answer some questions about your eating habits? You see, we're doing a nationwide survey on diet and we need . . . you would? Oh, that's most kind of you. Now if you could just give me your name and address and tell me briefly what you have for breakfast, lunch and dinner. It won't take a moment, I assure you.

**10** No thanks, I couldn't possibly eat another thing. That was a really delicious meal. I don't know how you have the patience to cook such complicated meals. I usually pop out to the fish and chip shop or have a Chinese take-away when I'm on my own. It's quick and fairly cheap. It doesn't seem worth cooking for myself, somehow.

**11**

## A sizzling offer from Sullivans.

For the next few weeks two of you can wine and dine for less than a tenner.

Choose from a New York Strip, a great cut of steak, sizzled on the char grill. Or try the Steak Teriyaki – marinated to make this the most tender steak you've ever eaten.

Both steaks are served with a choice of jacket potato, shoestring fries or American wild rice. And to complete the meal, there's a FREE bottle of red or white Californian wine.

Remember to bring this coupon with you and hand it to the waitress when you order.

But hurry – this offer ends on 31st October 1985.

SULLIVANS, BEEHIVE LANE, ILFORD, ESSEX, TEL: 01-550 3361.

---

**STEAK AND A FREE BOTTLE OF WINE**

**JUST £9.98 FOR TWO**

When two people order their choice of a New York Strip or Steak Teryaki – they can also enjoy a FREE bottle of Red or White Californian wine* – and all for just £9.98 for two.

This offer is valid from 1st September to 31st October 1985 and excludes Saturday nights.

Please hand this voucher to the waitress when ordering.

Bill No. _____ Waitress Sig. _____

**THIS OFFER ENDS 31st OCTOBER 1985**

* Not applicable if under 18 years of age.

SULLIVANS, BEEHIVE LANE, ILFORD, ESSEX, TEL: 01-550 3361.

*Interview Exercises*

**12**     You and your wife/husband are giving a New Year Party for 30 people and you have asked a friend to help you with the catering. Plan the food and drink for the party keeping in mind any special dietary needs of the guests.

## ADVENTURE; TAKING RISKS

**13**

**14**     Johnny Weevil was seriously injured today on the film set for the new adventure film *Fire Killer* at Elmtree Studios. In one scene Johnny had to jump from the third floor of a blazing building but, according to a spokesman for the film company, the building burnt at such a rapid rate that Johnny was trapped before he could jump. He was rescued by firemen and taken to hospital, where he is being treated for extensive burns.

*Interview Exercises*

**15** When I was at school – I think I must've been about nine or ten years old – we used to play a game called 'daredevil'. I remember someone dared me to climb up the fire escape onto the school roof. Well, I did it when there were no teachers around to see me, the only problem was I couldn't get down again! I was scared stiff and of course I had to wait until a teacher came to fetch me!

**16** And live from the Holmenkollen in Oslo we bring you this year's spectacular ski-jump championships. Those of you who have watched the competition in previous years may remember the tragic death last year of Steve Williams who crashed to his death seconds after he had left the ski-jump when one of his skis came loose. Let's hope this year's competition will be free of any similar accidents.

**17**

**Alton Towers**

## Science in action

### "Britain's only world-rated leisure park"

Many of the rides at Alton Towers allow some of the major laws of physics to be experienced. We have introduced a physics trail to encourage pupils to think about the physical concepts behind the ride they are trying. It takes as its starting point the fact that many of our most exciting rides are marvels of modern engineering which provide a practical demonstration of some of the basic principles of physics.

Your pupils are directed to rides like the Corkscrew and Log Flume where they can experience for themselves the laws of physics in action – and at the same time have lots of fun.

CORKSCREW
Pupils can experience first hand the centrifugal and G-forces of the ride that has become a nationwide favourite. (Maximum height 23m, top speed 70kph, G-force exerted 3.1.)

*Interview Exercises*

## 18

It's impossible to cover the whole of Alton Towers in one day. Using the map and the key how would you plan to spend a day at Alton Towers? What would you choose to do? Why would you choose these particular activities? Be prepared to discuss your ideas with the examiner or the group, pointing out on the map the things you would want to do and the route you would take.

KEY

1 **Towers Street**
   Visitor Information
   Toy Fair
   Bagshaw's Restaurant

2 **Kiddies' Kingdom**
   Suspension Bridge
   Spider Mountain
   Building Site

3 **Fantasy World**
   Black Hole
   Miniature Golf
   Fun Bouncer
   Alpine Bobsleigh
   Cine 2000

4 **Talbot Street**
   Adventure Railway
   Fun Centre
   Wild Life Museum

5 **Festival Park**
   Corkscrew Rollercoaster
   Ferris Wheel
   Wave Swinger

6 **Gardens**
   Rock Garden
   Chinese Temple

7 **Aqualand**
   Grand Canyon Rapid Rides
   Cable Cars
   Aquarium
   Rowing Boats

8 **The Towers**
   Towers Gift Shop
   Model Railway
   Viewing Platform

[104]

*Interview Exercises*

Towers Street

Kiddies Kingdom

Fantasy World

Talbot Street

The Towers

**T** Toilets
**◎** Film Shops
**C** Public Telephones
**DT** Special Toilets for the disabled
**✚** First aid, lost children and baby feeding facilities

[105]

*Interview Exercises*

## TRAVEL AND TRANSPORT

**19**

**20** Passengers are requested to report to coach departure at town terminal or at check-in counter at the airport at times stated in the SAS worldwide timetable. The times for coach departure are given as guidelines and do not relieve the passengers from the responsibility of being at the airport before the prescribed check-in time.

**21** A police car was involved in a head-on collision with a petrol tanker in the city centre in the early hours of Monday morning. According to eyewitnesses the driver of the petrol tanker was exceeding the speed limit at the time of the crash. Police are checking the driver's log book to try and establish his delivery schedule. A spokesman for the company denied that petrol tanker drivers are required to work after eight in the evening.

*Interview Exercises*

**22** Some mornings I don't hear my alarm go off and if I oversleep it means a terrible rush to catch my bus. I jump into my clothes, grab an apple and tear out of the house. I slam the front door, which makes my parents furious, and race down the street to the bus stop. I'm usually so out of breath I can't even ask the driver for my fare!

**23**

### HOTEL SIMONOV ZALIV

One of the most appealing features of the Simonov Zaliv is the lovely view it offers across the bay to the fishing harbour of Izola and beyond towards the Italian coastline. Standing in large, luxuriant gardens, its two buildings are less than 300 yards from the beach where the grill bar provides light lunches and snacks in high season and pedalos can be hired. Izola is about ten minutes away.
- pool (closed July and August); terraces and gardens; beach bar with grill
- reception lounge; bar
- dining room in separate building near the beach; main meals waiter service with choice of menu; à la carte menu available
- three tennis courts (equipment for hire); table-tennis; crazy-golf
- TV; cards and chess
- discotheque; dancing three times a week to live music
- cots available

### HOTEL DELFIN

The Delfin is a very stylish, modern hotel on the seafront with fine views across the bay to Izola's charming fishing harbour and guests can bathe from a rocky beach just a few yards from the hotel. Surrounded by lush gardens, the Delfin is particularly popular with those seeking a quieter holiday and the hotel offers special health and beauty treatments. The countryside is pleasant for quiet strolls and you can reach the little town of Izola in about ten minutes.
- indoor pool; sun terraces; gardens; seafront snack bar (open in high season)
- air-conditioned public rooms; pretty pine-furnished bar
- airy dining room; main meals waiter service with choice of menu; à la carte menu available
- TV; bowls
- dancing every evening on terrace (in high season)
- hairdresser; massage and beauty treatments available

[107]

*Interview Exercises*

**24** You are planning a long-distance journey, for example London – Moscow, Paris – Beijing, a tour within India etc., which will take at least two weeks. Discuss some of the things you would need to consider when planning such a journey. What are the problems? What do you need to know in advance? What would you take with you? Make a list of your points and try to draw up a plan.

## ENTERTAINMENT

**25**

**26** Television is the most influential of all the media. A single television programme has more impact than radio and the printed word put together. For this reason alone TV producers and programme makers have a responsibility to the general public to ensure the highest possible standards. This applies to all aspects of television but perhaps especially to those programmes which are aimed at children and young people.

*Interview Exercises*

**27** *Magic Circles 3301* is the latest offering from the Hollywood film studios. The film was made with a budget of three and a half million dollars, half of which was spent on constructing the most elaborate space age scenery ever. 'It took a hundred and twenty workmen two years to complete,' said the producer Tom Watson, 'and my guess is it will take about two weeks to pull down once we've finished shooting.'

**28** Before Christmas I was employed by a telephone sales company working from 7.30 – 10.30 at night. I had lists of people whom I had to ring up to follow up business contacts. I was really concerned at the number of young children who answered the phone and said their parents were watching television. When I asked whether I could speak to one of their parents I was invariably told 'no'.

**29**

A delightful introduction to the magic of music

**Sinbad and the Wizard Eagle**

AND OTHER STORIES FROM THE WORLD OF GREAT MUSIC BY

**Ann Rachlin**

Nine marvellous tales based on great music by famous composers, including Bach, Rimsky-Korsakov, Prokofiev and Gershwin.

**FUNTASIA 86**

Make a New Year resolution to bring your family into the magical world of great music...

Music And Stories For Children
Live On Stage At The Barbican
with ANN RACHLIN and the
LONDON SYMPHONY ORCHESTRA

*Interview Exercises*

# 30

## 10.30
### Food for Thought
MARION BOWMAN
BRIAN J FORD
**THE DIET REVOLUTION**

Repeated series looking at the part food plays in our lives, where it comes from, what's in it and what it does to us. This first programme charts the major changes in our eating habits over the past 200 years. For a free leaflet, send an sae to address 1, page 65.  ‡
CAMERA CHRIS O'DELL
SERIES SUPERVISOR
SUE TRAMONTINI
DIRECTOR/SERIES EDITOR
CHRIS HAWS
EXECUTIVE PRODUCER
DOUGLAS KENTISH
*Illustra Television in association with the Health Education Council*

## 10.30 Midweek Sport Special
BRIAN MOORE

The day's top action, news and personalities, including snooker, football and tennis.
PRODUCER LEWIS WILLIAMS
EXECUTIVE PRODUCER
BOB BURROWS
EDITOR PHIL KING
*Independent Television Sport Production*

You and your friend(s) disagree over which television programme to watch this evening. Try to persuade them to change their mind as you have been looking forward to this programme all day.

# Optional Reading

GRAHAM GREENE: *The Third Man*

**31**

**32** He said, 'I've been with the British police. They are satisfied I didn't do it. But I've learned everything from them. Harry was in a racket – a bad racket.' He said hopelessly, 'He was no good at all. We were both wrong.'

'You'd better tell me,' Anna said. She sat down on the bed and he told her, swaying slightly beside the table where her typescript part still lay open at the first page.

*Optional Reading*

**33** He had only to rise once again through the ground, walk fifty yards, bring Martins back with him, and sink again into the obscurity of the sewers. He had no idea that this method of evasion was known to us: he probably knew that one patrol of the sewer police ended before midnight, and the next did not start till two, and so at midnight Martins sat in the little cold cafe in sight of the kiosk, drinking coffee after coffee.

**34** He stared down into his glass, drained what was left, and said, 'It's a damned shame to think of him dying the way he did.'
'It was the best thing that ever happened to him,' I said.
He didn't take in my meaning at once: he was a little hazy with his drinks. 'The best thing?'
'Yes.'
'You mean there wasn't any pain?'
'He was lucky in that way, too.'

**35** Someone gave her a hand and she looked round with a lost hopeless gaze at this crowd of strangers. If there were friends there she did not recognize them, looking from face to face. Martins bent as she passed, fumbling at his shoelace, but looking up from the ground he saw at his own eyes' level the scrutinizing cold-blooded gnome-gaze of little Hansel.

**36** The examiner will ask you to discuss one or more of the following topics:

1 the story in its post-war Vienna setting

2 the way the story is told by Calloway

3 the way various characters hide their knowledge of the truth (Kurtz, Koch, Martins himself)

4 details of some striking scenery (Sewers, Theatre, Prater)

5 the significance of the title

6 whether the story is better as a film or a book

## G. B. SHAW: *Arms and the Man*

**37**

**38**
– Be warned in time, Louka: mend your manners. I know the mistress. She is so grand that she never dreams that any servant could dare be disrespectful to her; but if she once suspects that you are defying her, out you go.
– I do defy her. I will defy her. What do I care for her?
– If you quarrel with the family, I never can marry you. It's the same as if you quarrelled with me!

*Optional Reading*

**39**
– Remember: 'I'm a soldier. Now what are the two things that happen to a soldier so often that he comes to think nothing of them? One is hearing people tell lies: the other is getting his life saved in all sorts of ways by all sorts of people.
– And so he becomes a creature incapable of faith and of gratitude.
– Do you like gratitude? I don't. If pity is akin to love, gratitude is akin to the other thing.

**40**
– I don't believe in going too far with these modern customs. All this washing can't be good for the health: it's not natural. There was an Englishman at Philipopolis who used to wet himself all over with cold water every morning when he got up. Disgusting! It all comes from the English: their climate makes them so dirty that they have to be perpetually washing themselves.

**41**
– Yes: I was only a prosaic little coward. Oh, to think that it was all true! That he is just as splendid and noble as he looks! That the world is really a glorious world for women who can see its glory and men who can act its romance! What happiness! What unspeakable fulfilment!

**42**
The examiner will ask you to discuss one or more of the following topics:

1 Raina's romantic nature

2 the significance of the chocolates

3 the hiding of Bluntschli

# Acknowledgements

The University of Cambridge Local Examinations Syndicate and the publishers are grateful to the following for permission to reproduce texts and illustrations. It has not been possible to identify sources of all the material used and in such cases the publishers would welcome information from copyright owners.

A. D. Peters & Company Ltd for the extract from *The Realms of Gold* by Margaret Drabble on pp.4–5; Penguin Books Ltd for the adapted blurb from *Claudius The God* by Robert Graves on p.8; Hodder & Stoughton Ltd and John Farquharson Ltd for the extract from *Smiley's People* by John le Carré on pp.23–4; Shire Publications Ltd and Nigel Harvey for the extract from *Discovering Farm Livestock* by Nigel Harvey on p.25; The Yorkshire Post for the extract from *Trains to Nowhere* by Alan Whitehouse on pp.62–3; Edward Arnold for the extract from *Pastoral Care in Schools and Colleges* by K. David and J. Cowley on p.64; the Paints Division of ICI International Ltd for the Dulux Paint advertisement on p.65; A. P. Watt Ltd for the extract from *Politics is for People* by Shirley Williams on pp.81–2; Anchor Hotels for the 'Breakaways' competition on p.84; Barnaby's Picture Library for the photograph on p.98; the Meteorological Office for the weather information on p.99; Nigel Luckhurst for the photographs on pp.100 and 106; Imperial Inns and Taverns Ltd for the advertisement for Sullivan's 'Steak Meal Offer' on p.101; Associated Press Ltd for the photograph on p.102; Alton Towers Ltd for the photograph, text and map on pp.103, 104 and 105; Thomson Holidays Ltd for the photographs and text on p.107; Granada Television Ltd for the photograph on p.108; The London Symphony Orchestra and EMI Records Ltd for the leaflet on p.109; TVTimes for the texts on p.110; Paul Hogarth for the illustration from the front cover of *The Third Man/The Fallen Idol* by Graham Greene, Penguin Books Ltd, 1971 on p.111; William Heinemann and The Bodley Head for the extracts from *The Third Man* by Graham Greene on pp.111–12; Jon Sheffield for the programme cover design *Arms and the Man* on p.113; The Society of Authors on behalf of the Bernard Shaw estate for the extracts from *Arms and the Man* by G. B. Shaw on pp.113–14.

The texts of the Edinburgh Leisureline and Stratford Leisureline are re-recorded and reproduced by kind permission of British Telecom and the Tourist Information Centre, Stratford-on-Avon.

H

# OBJECTIVE TEST ANSWER SHEET

**FOR SUPERVISOR USE ONLY**
Shade this lozenge ▭
if the candidate is
absent or was withdrawn.

Subject/Paper No.
Subject Name

Centre/Candidate Number .................................................................................

Candidate Name ...............................................................................................

If your Centre/Candidate Number
and Name are not shown, please
enter them on the dotted lines.

### A. GENERAL INSTRUCTIONS TO THE CANDIDATE

1. TELL THE SUPERVISOR IMMEDIATELY IF YOUR CENTRE/CANDIDATE NUMBER OR NAME ARE INCORRECT.

2. IF THE INFORMATION ABOVE IS CORRECT, PLEASE SIGN HERE. ........................................................................................

3. USE A SOFT HB PENCIL ONLY FOR YOUR ANSWERS ON THIS SHEET.
   DO NOT USE INK OR BALL POINT PEN.

### INSTRUCTIONS FOR RECORDING ANSWERS

1. SUGGESTED ANSWERS TO EACH QUESTION ARE GIVEN IN THE QUESTION PAPER. CHOOSE AN ANSWER AND SHADE THE SPACE BELOW THE CORRESPONDING LETTER ON THIS SHEET THUS $\underline{A}$

2. ERRORS – THOROUGHLY RUB OUT ANY ERRORS WITH A CLEAN RUBBER. LEAVE NO SMUDGES.

|    | A | B | C | D |    | A | B | C | D |
|----|---|---|---|---|----|---|---|---|---|
| 1  | ▭ | ▭ | ▭ | ▭ | 21 | ▭ | ▭ | ▭ | ▭ |
| 2  | ▭ | ▭ | ▭ | ▭ | 22 | ▭ | ▭ | ▭ | ▭ |
| 3  | ▭ | ▭ | ▭ | ▭ | 23 | ▭ | ▭ | ▭ | ▭ |
| 4  | ▭ | ▭ | ▭ | ▭ | 24 | ▭ | ▭ | ▭ | ▭ |
| 5  | ▭ | ▭ | ▭ | ▭ | 25 | ▭ | ▭ | ▭ | ▭ |
| 6  | ▭ | ▭ | ▭ | ▭ | 26 | ▭ | ▭ | ▭ | ▭ |
| 7  | ▭ | ▭ | ▭ | ▭ | 27 | ▭ | ▭ | ▭ | ▭ |
| 8  | ▭ | ▭ | ▭ | ▭ | 28 | ▭ | ▭ | ▭ | ▭ |
| 9  | ▭ | ▭ | ▭ | ▭ | 29 | ▭ | ▭ | ▭ | ▭ |
| 10 | ▭ | ▭ | ▭ | ▭ | 30 | ▭ | ▭ | ▭ | ▭ |
| 11 | ▭ | ▭ | ▭ | ▭ | 31 | ▭ | ▭ | ▭ | ▭ |
| 12 | ▭ | ▭ | ▭ | ▭ | 32 | ▭ | ▭ | ▭ | ▭ |
| 13 | ▭ | ▭ | ▭ | ▭ | 33 | ▭ | ▭ | ▭ | ▭ |
| 14 | ▭ | ▭ | ▭ | ▭ | 34 | ▭ | ▭ | ▭ | ▭ |
| 15 | ▭ | ▭ | ▭ | ▭ | 25 | ▭ | ▭ | ▭ | ▭ |
| 16 | ▭ | ▭ | ▭ | ▭ | 26 | ▭ | ▭ | ▭ | ▭ |
| 17 | ▭ | ▭ | ▭ | ▭ | 27 | ▭ | ▭ | ▭ | ▭ |
| 18 | ▭ | ▭ | ▭ | ▭ | 28 | ▭ | ▭ | ▭ | ▭ |
| 19 | ▭ | ▭ | ▭ | ▭ | 39 | ▭ | ▭ | ▭ | ▭ |
| 20 | ▭ | ▭ | ▭ | ▭ | 40 | ▭ | ▭ | ▭ | ▭ |

H

## OBJECTIVE TEST ANSWER SHEET

Subject/Paper No.
Subject Name

**FOR SUPERVISOR USE ONLY**
Shade this lozenge ▭
if the candidate is
absent or was withdrawn.

Centre/Candidate Number ..............................................................................

Candidate Name ..............................................................................

If your Centre/Candidate Number and Name are not shown, please enter them on the dotted lines.

### A. GENERAL INSTRUCTIONS TO THE CANDIDATE

1. TELL THE SUPERVISOR IMMEDIATELY IF YOUR CENTRE/CANDIDATE NUMBER OR NAME ARE INCORRECT.

2. IF THE INFORMATION ABOVE IS CORRECT, PLEASE SIGN HERE. ..............................................................................

3. USE A SOFT HB PENCIL ONLY FOR YOUR ANSWERS ON THIS SHEET.
   DO NOT USE INK OR BALL POINT PEN.

### INSTRUCTIONS FOR RECORDING ANSWERS

1. SUGGESTED ANSWERS TO EACH QUESTION ARE GIVEN IN THE QUESTION PAPER. CHOOSE AN ANSWER AND SHADE THE SPACE BELOW THE CORRESPONDING LETTER ON THIS SHEET THUS ▲

2. ERRORS – THOROUGHLY RUB OUT ANY ERRORS WITH A CLEAN RUBBER. LEAVE NO SMUDGES.

|    | A | B | C | D |    | A | B | C | D |
|----|---|---|---|---|----|---|---|---|---|
| 1  | ▢ | ▢ | ▢ | ▢ | 21 | ▢ | ▢ | ▢ | ▢ |
| 2  | ▢ | ▢ | ▢ | ▢ | 22 | ▢ | ▢ | ▢ | ▢ |
| 3  | ▢ | ▢ | ▢ | ▢ | 23 | ▢ | ▢ | ▢ | ▢ |
| 4  | ▢ | ▢ | ▢ | ▢ | 24 | ▢ | ▢ | ▢ | ▢ |
| 5  | ▢ | ▢ | ▢ | ▢ | 25 | ▢ | ▢ | ▢ | ▢ |
| 6  | ▢ | ▢ | ▢ | ▢ | 26 | ▢ | ▢ | ▢ | ▢ |
| 7  | ▢ | ▢ | ▢ | ▢ | 27 | ▢ | ▢ | ▢ | ▢ |
| 8  | ▢ | ▢ | ▢ | ▢ | 28 | ▢ | ▢ | ▢ | ▢ |
| 9  | ▢ | ▢ | ▢ | ▢ | 29 | ▢ | ▢ | ▢ | ▢ |
| 10 | ▢ | ▢ | ▢ | ▢ | 30 | ▢ | ▢ | ▢ | ▢ |
| 11 | ▢ | ▢ | ▢ | ▢ | 31 | ▢ | ▢ | ▢ | ▢ |
| 12 | ▢ | ▢ | ▢ | ▢ | 32 | ▢ | ▢ | ▢ | ▢ |
| 13 | ▢ | ▢ | ▢ | ▢ | 33 | ▢ | ▢ | ▢ | ▢ |
| 14 | ▢ | ▢ | ▢ | ▢ | 34 | ▢ | ▢ | ▢ | ▢ |
| 15 | ▢ | ▢ | ▢ | ▢ | 25 | ▢ | ▢ | ▢ | ▢ |
| 16 | ▢ | ▢ | ▢ | ▢ | 26 | ▢ | ▢ | ▢ | ▢ |
| 17 | ▢ | ▢ | ▢ | ▢ | 27 | ▢ | ▢ | ▢ | ▢ |
| 18 | ▢ | ▢ | ▢ | ▢ | 28 | ▢ | ▢ | ▢ | ▢ |
| 19 | ▢ | ▢ | ▢ | ▢ | 39 | ▢ | ▢ | ▢ | ▢ |
| 20 | ▢ | ▢ | ▢ | ▢ | 40 | ▢ | ▢ | ▢ | ▢ |

H

## OBJECTIVE TEST ANSWER SHEET

Subject/Paper No.
Subject Name

**FOR SUPERVISOR USE ONLY**
Shade this lozenge ▭
if the candidate is
absent or was withdrawn.

Centre/Candidate Number .......................................................................

Candidate Name .......................................................................

If your Centre/Candidate Number and Name are not shown, please enter them on the dotted lines.

**A. GENERAL INSTRUCTIONS TO THE CANDIDATE**

1. TELL THE SUPERVISOR IMMEDIATELY IF YOUR CENTRE/CANDIDATE NUMBER OR NAME ARE INCORRECT.

2. IF THE INFORMATION ABOVE IS CORRECT, PLEASE SIGN HERE. ..........................................................................................

3. USE A SOFT HB PENCIL ONLY FOR YOUR ANSWERS ON THIS SHEET.
   DO NOT USE INK OR BALL POINT PEN.

**INSTRUCTIONS FOR RECORDING ANSWERS**

1. SUGGESTED ANSWERS TO EACH QUESTION ARE GIVEN IN THE QUESTION PAPER. CHOOSE AN ANSWER AND SHADE THE SPACE BELOW THE CORRESPONDING LETTER ON THIS SHEET THUS $\underline{A}$

2. ERRORS – THOROUGHLY RUB OUT ANY ERRORS WITH A CLEAN RUBBER. LEAVE NO SMUDGES.

|    | A | B | C | D |    | A | B | C | D |
|----|---|---|---|---|----|---|---|---|---|
| 1  | ▭ | ▭ | ▭ | ▭ | 21 | ▭ | ▭ | ▭ | ▭ |
| 2  | ▭ | ▭ | ▭ | ▭ | 22 | ▭ | ▭ | ▭ | ▭ |
| 3  | ▭ | ▭ | ▭ | ▭ | 23 | ▭ | ▭ | ▭ | ▭ |
| 4  | ▭ | ▭ | ▭ | ▭ | 24 | ▭ | ▭ | ▭ | ▭ |
| 5  | ▭ | ▭ | ▭ | ▭ | 25 | ▭ | ▭ | ▭ | ▭ |
| 6  | ▭ | ▭ | ▭ | ▭ | 26 | ▭ | ▭ | ▭ | ▭ |
| 7  | ▭ | ▭ | ▭ | ▭ | 27 | ▭ | ▭ | ▭ | ▭ |
| 8  | ▭ | ▭ | ▭ | ▭ | 28 | ▭ | ▭ | ▭ | ▭ |
| 9  | ▭ | ▭ | ▭ | ▭ | 29 | ▭ | ▭ | ▭ | ▭ |
| 10 | ▭ | ▭ | ▭ | ▭ | 30 | ▭ | ▭ | ▭ | ▭ |
| 11 | ▭ | ▭ | ▭ | ▭ | 31 | ▭ | ▭ | ▭ | ▭ |
| 12 | ▭ | ▭ | ▭ | ▭ | 32 | ▭ | ▭ | ▭ | ▭ |
| 13 | ▭ | ▭ | ▭ | ▭ | 33 | ▭ | ▭ | ▭ | ▭ |
| 14 | ▭ | ▭ | ▭ | ▭ | 34 | ▭ | ▭ | ▭ | ▭ |
| 15 | ▭ | ▭ | ▭ | ▭ | 25 | ▭ | ▭ | ▭ | ▭ |
| 16 | ▭ | ▭ | ▭ | ▭ | 26 | ▭ | ▭ | ▭ | ▭ |
| 17 | ▭ | ▭ | ▭ | ▭ | 27 | ▭ | ▭ | ▭ | ▭ |
| 18 | ▭ | ▭ | ▭ | ▭ | 28 | ▭ | ▭ | ▭ | ▭ |
| 19 | ▭ | ▭ | ▭ | ▭ | 39 | ▭ | ▭ | ▭ | ▭ |
| 20 | ▭ | ▭ | ▭ | ▭ | 40 | ▭ | ▭ | ▭ | ▭ |

H

## OBJECTIVE TEST ANSWER SHEET

Subject/Paper No.
Subject Name

Centre/Candidate Number ................................................................................

Candidate Name ................................................................................

**FOR SUPERVISOR USE ONLY**
Shade this lozenge ▭
if the candidate is
absent or was withdrawn.

If your Centre/Candidate Number and Name are not shown, please enter them on the dotted lines.

### A. GENERAL INSTRUCTIONS TO THE CANDIDATE

1. TELL THE SUPERVISOR IMMEDIATELY IF YOUR CENTRE/CANDIDATE NUMBER OR NAME ARE INCORRECT.
2. IF THE INFORMATION ABOVE IS CORRECT, PLEASE SIGN HERE. ................................................................................
3. USE A SOFT HB PENCIL ONLY FOR YOUR ANSWERS ON THIS SHEET. DO NOT USE INK OR BALL POINT PEN.

### INSTRUCTIONS FOR RECORDING ANSWERS

1. SUGGESTED ANSWERS TO EACH QUESTION ARE GIVEN IN THE QUESTION PAPER. CHOOSE AN ANSWER AND SHADE THE SPACE BELOW THE CORRESPONDING LETTER ON THIS SHEET THUS ▬
2. ERRORS – THOROUGHLY RUB OUT ANY ERRORS WITH A CLEAN RUBBER. LEAVE NO SMUDGES.

|    | A | B | C | D |    | A | B | C | D |
|----|---|---|---|---|----|---|---|---|---|
| 1  | ▭ | ▭ | ▭ | ▭ | 21 | ▭ | ▭ | ▭ | ▭ |
| 2  | ▭ | ▭ | ▭ | ▭ | 22 | ▭ | ▭ | ▭ | ▭ |
| 3  | ▭ | ▭ | ▭ | ▭ | 23 | ▭ | ▭ | ▭ | ▭ |
| 4  | ▭ | ▭ | ▭ | ▭ | 24 | ▭ | ▭ | ▭ | ▭ |
| 5  | ▭ | ▭ | ▭ | ▭ | 25 | ▭ | ▭ | ▭ | ▭ |
| 6  | ▭ | ▭ | ▭ | ▭ | 26 | ▭ | ▭ | ▭ | ▭ |
| 7  | ▭ | ▭ | ▭ | ▭ | 27 | ▭ | ▭ | ▭ | ▭ |
| 8  | ▭ | ▭ | ▭ | ▭ | 28 | ▭ | ▭ | ▭ | ▭ |
| 9  | ▭ | ▭ | ▭ | ▭ | 29 | ▭ | ▭ | ▭ | ▭ |
| 10 | ▭ | ▭ | ▭ | ▭ | 30 | ▭ | ▭ | ▭ | ▭ |
| 11 | ▭ | ▭ | ▭ | ▭ | 31 | ▭ | ▭ | ▭ | ▭ |
| 12 | ▭ | ▭ | ▭ | ▭ | 32 | ▭ | ▭ | ▭ | ▭ |
| 13 | ▭ | ▭ | ▭ | ▭ | 33 | ▭ | ▭ | ▭ | ▭ |
| 14 | ▭ | ▭ | ▭ | ▭ | 34 | ▭ | ▭ | ▭ | ▭ |
| 15 | ▭ | ▭ | ▭ | ▭ | 25 | ▭ | ▭ | ▭ | ▭ |
| 16 | ▭ | ▭ | ▭ | ▭ | 26 | ▭ | ▭ | ▭ | ▭ |
| 17 | ▭ | ▭ | ▭ | ▭ | 27 | ▭ | ▭ | ▭ | ▭ |
| 18 | ▭ | ▭ | ▭ | ▭ | 28 | ▭ | ▭ | ▭ | ▭ |
| 19 | ▭ | ▭ | ▭ | ▭ | 39 | ▭ | ▭ | ▭ | ▭ |
| 20 | ▭ | ▭ | ▭ | ▭ | 40 | ▭ | ▭ | ▭ | ▭ |

H

**OBJECTIVE TEST ANSWER SHEET**

**FOR SUPERVISOR USE ONLY**
Shade this lozenge ☐
if the candidate is
absent or was withdrawn.

Subject/Paper No.
Subject Name

Centre/Candidate Number .........................................................................

Candidate Name ........................................................................................

If your Centre/Candidate Number
and Name are not shown, please
enter them on the dotted lines.

**A. GENERAL INSTRUCTIONS TO THE CANDIDATE**

1. TELL THE SUPERVISOR IMMEDIATELY IF YOUR CENTRE/CANDIDATE NUMBER OR NAME ARE INCORRECT.

2. IF THE INFORMATION ABOVE IS CORRECT, PLEASE SIGN HERE. ................................................................................

3. USE A SOFT HB PENCIL ONLY FOR YOUR ANSWERS ON THIS SHEET.
   DO NOT USE INK OR BALL POINT PEN.

**INSTRUCTIONS FOR RECORDING ANSWERS**

1. SUGGESTED ANSWERS TO EACH QUESTION ARE GIVEN IN THE QUESTION PAPER. CHOOSE AN ANSWER AND SHADE THE SPACE BELOW THE CORRESPONDING LETTER ON THIS SHEET THUS **A̲**

2. ERRORS — THOROUGHLY RUB OUT ANY ERRORS WITH A CLEAN RUBBER. LEAVE NO SMUDGES.

|    | A | B | C | D |    | A | B | C | D |
|----|---|---|---|---|----|---|---|---|---|
| 1  | ☐ | ☐ | ☐ | ☐ | 21 | ☐ | ☐ | ☐ | ☐ |
| 2  | ☐ | ☐ | ☐ | ☐ | 22 | ☐ | ☐ | ☐ | ☐ |
| 3  | ☐ | ☐ | ☐ | ☐ | 23 | ☐ | ☐ | ☐ | ☐ |
| 4  | ☐ | ☐ | ☐ | ☐ | 24 | ☐ | ☐ | ☐ | ☐ |
| 5  | ☐ | ☐ | ☐ | ☐ | 25 | ☐ | ☐ | ☐ | ☐ |
| 6  | ☐ | ☐ | ☐ | ☐ | 26 | ☐ | ☐ | ☐ | ☐ |
| 7  | ☐ | ☐ | ☐ | ☐ | 27 | ☐ | ☐ | ☐ | ☐ |
| 8  | ☐ | ☐ | ☐ | ☐ | 28 | ☐ | ☐ | ☐ | ☐ |
| 9  | ☐ | ☐ | ☐ | ☐ | 29 | ☐ | ☐ | ☐ | ☐ |
| 10 | ☐ | ☐ | ☐ | ☐ | 30 | ☐ | ☐ | ☐ | ☐ |
| 11 | ☐ | ☐ | ☐ | ☐ | 31 | ☐ | ☐ | ☐ | ☐ |
| 12 | ☐ | ☐ | ☐ | ☐ | 32 | ☐ | ☐ | ☐ | ☐ |
| 13 | ☐ | ☐ | ☐ | ☐ | 33 | ☐ | ☐ | ☐ | ☐ |
| 14 | ☐ | ☐ | ☐ | ☐ | 34 | ☐ | ☐ | ☐ | ☐ |
| 15 | ☐ | ☐ | ☐ | ☐ | 25 | ☐ | ☐ | ☐ | ☐ |
| 16 | ☐ | ☐ | ☐ | ☐ | 26 | ☐ | ☐ | ☐ | ☐ |
| 17 | ☐ | ☐ | ☐ | ☐ | 27 | ☐ | ☐ | ☐ | ☐ |
| 18 | ☐ | ☐ | ☐ | ☐ | 28 | ☐ | ☐ | ☐ | ☐ |
| 19 | ☐ | ☐ | ☐ | ☐ | 39 | ☐ | ☐ | ☐ | ☐ |
| 20 | ☐ | ☐ | ☐ | ☐ | 40 | ☐ | ☐ | ☐ | ☐ |

H                    **OBJECTIVE TEST ANSWER SHEET**

**FOR SUPERVISOR USE ONLY**
Shade this lozenge ▭
if the candidate is
absent or was withdrawn.

Subject/Paper No.
Subject Name

Centre/Candidate Number ..................................................................

Candidate Name ..................................................................

If your Centre/Candidate Number and Name are not shown, please enter them on the dotted lines.

### A. GENERAL INSTRUCTIONS TO THE CANDIDATE

1. TELL THE SUPERVISOR IMMEDIATELY IF YOUR CENTRE/CANDIDATE NUMBER OR NAME ARE INCORRECT.
2. IF THE INFORMATION ABOVE IS CORRECT, PLEASE SIGN HERE. ..................................................................
3. USE A SOFT HB PENCIL ONLY FOR YOUR ANSWERS ON THIS SHEET. DO NOT USE INK OR BALL POINT PEN.

### INSTRUCTIONS FOR RECORDING ANSWERS

1. SUGGESTED ANSWERS TO EACH QUESTION ARE GIVEN IN THE QUESTION PAPER. CHOOSE AN ANSWER AND SHADE THE SPACE BELOW THE CORRESPONDING LETTER ON THIS SHEET THUS ▬
2. ERRORS – THOROUGHLY RUB OUT ANY ERRORS WITH A CLEAN RUBBER. LEAVE NO SMUDGES.

|    | A | B | C | D |    | A | B | C | D |
|----|---|---|---|---|----|---|---|---|---|
| 1  | ▭ | ▭ | ▭ | ▭ | 21 | ▭ | ▭ | ▭ | ▭ |
| 2  | ▭ | ▭ | ▭ | ▭ | 22 | ▭ | ▭ | ▭ | ▭ |
| 3  | ▭ | ▭ | ▭ | ▭ | 23 | ▭ | ▭ | ▭ | ▭ |
| 4  | ▭ | ▭ | ▭ | ▭ | 24 | ▭ | ▭ | ▭ | ▭ |
| 5  | ▭ | ▭ | ▭ | ▭ | 25 | ▭ | ▭ | ▭ | ▭ |
| 6  | ▭ | ▭ | ▭ | ▭ | 26 | ▭ | ▭ | ▭ | ▭ |
| 7  | ▭ | ▭ | ▭ | ▭ | 27 | ▭ | ▭ | ▭ | ▭ |
| 8  | ▭ | ▭ | ▭ | ▭ | 28 | ▭ | ▭ | ▭ | ▭ |
| 9  | ▭ | ▭ | ▭ | ▭ | 29 | ▭ | ▭ | ▭ | ▭ |
| 10 | ▭ | ▭ | ▭ | ▭ | 30 | ▭ | ▭ | ▭ | ▭ |
| 11 | ▭ | ▭ | ▭ | ▭ | 31 | ▭ | ▭ | ▭ | ▭ |
| 12 | ▭ | ▭ | ▭ | ▭ | 32 | ▭ | ▭ | ▭ | ▭ |
| 13 | ▭ | ▭ | ▭ | ▭ | 33 | ▭ | ▭ | ▭ | ▭ |
| 14 | ▭ | ▭ | ▭ | ▭ | 34 | ▭ | ▭ | ▭ | ▭ |
| 15 | ▭ | ▭ | ▭ | ▭ | 25 | ▭ | ▭ | ▭ | ▭ |
| 16 | ▭ | ▭ | ▭ | ▭ | 26 | ▭ | ▭ | ▭ | ▭ |
| 17 | ▭ | ▭ | ▭ | ▭ | 27 | ▭ | ▭ | ▭ | ▭ |
| 18 | ▭ | ▭ | ▭ | ▭ | 28 | ▭ | ▭ | ▭ | ▭ |
| 19 | ▭ | ▭ | ▭ | ▭ | 39 | ▭ | ▭ | ▭ | ▭ |
| 20 | ▭ | ▭ | ▭ | ▭ | 40 | ▭ | ▭ | ▭ | ▭ |

H                    **OBJECTIVE TEST ANSWER SHEET**

Subject/Paper No.
Subject Name

**FOR SUPERVISOR USE ONLY**
Shade this lozenge ▭
if the candidate is
absent or was withdrawn.

Centre/Candidate Number ..................................................................

Candidate Name ................................................................................

If your Centre/Candidate Number
and Name are not shown, please
enter them on the dotted lines.

**A.    GENERAL INSTRUCTIONS TO THE CANDIDATE**

1. TELL THE SUPERVISOR IMMEDIATELY IF YOUR CENTRE/CANDIDATE NUMBER OR NAME ARE INCORRECT.
2. IF THE INFORMATION ABOVE IS CORRECT, PLEASE SIGN HERE. ...........................................................................
3. USE A SOFT HB PENCIL ONLY FOR YOUR ANSWERS ON THIS SHEET.
   DO NOT USE INK OR BALL POINT PEN.

**INSTRUCTIONS FOR RECORDING ANSWERS**

1. SUGGESTED ANSWERS TO EACH QUESTION ARE GIVEN IN THE QUESTION PAPER. CHOOSE AN ANSWER AND SHADE THE SPACE BELOW THE CORRESPONDING LETTER ON THIS SHEET THUS ▬
2. ERRORS – THOROUGHLY RUB OUT ANY ERRORS WITH A CLEAN RUBBER. LEAVE NO SMUDGES.

|    | A | B | C | D |    | A | B | C | D |
|----|---|---|---|---|----|---|---|---|---|
| 1  | ▭ | ▭ | ▭ | ▭ | 21 | ▭ | ▭ | ▭ | ▭ |
| 2  | ▭ | ▭ | ▭ | ▭ | 22 | ▭ | ▭ | ▭ | ▭ |
| 3  | ▭ | ▭ | ▭ | ▭ | 23 | ▭ | ▭ | ▭ | ▭ |
| 4  | ▭ | ▭ | ▭ | ▭ | 24 | ▭ | ▭ | ▭ | ▭ |
| 5  | ▭ | ▭ | ▭ | ▭ | 25 | ▭ | ▭ | ▭ | ▭ |
| 6  | ▭ | ▭ | ▭ | ▭ | 26 | ▭ | ▭ | ▭ | ▭ |
| 7  | ▭ | ▭ | ▭ | ▭ | 27 | ▭ | ▭ | ▭ | ▭ |
| 8  | ▭ | ▭ | ▭ | ▭ | 28 | ▭ | ▭ | ▭ | ▭ |
| 9  | ▭ | ▭ | ▭ | ▭ | 29 | ▭ | ▭ | ▭ | ▭ |
| 10 | ▭ | ▭ | ▭ | ▭ | 30 | ▭ | ▭ | ▭ | ▭ |
| 11 | ▭ | ▭ | ▭ | ▭ | 31 | ▭ | ▭ | ▭ | ▭ |
| 12 | ▭ | ▭ | ▭ | ▭ | 32 | ▭ | ▭ | ▭ | ▭ |
| 13 | ▭ | ▭ | ▭ | ▭ | 33 | ▭ | ▭ | ▭ | ▭ |
| 14 | ▭ | ▭ | ▭ | ▭ | 34 | ▭ | ▭ | ▭ | ▭ |
| 15 | ▭ | ▭ | ▭ | ▭ | 25 | ▭ | ▭ | ▭ | ▭ |
| 16 | ▭ | ▭ | ▭ | ▭ | 26 | ▭ | ▭ | ▭ | ▭ |
| 17 | ▭ | ▭ | ▭ | ▭ | 27 | ▭ | ▭ | ▭ | ▭ |
| 18 | ▭ | ▭ | ▭ | ▭ | 28 | ▭ | ▭ | ▭ | ▭ |
| 19 | ▭ | ▭ | ▭ | ▭ | 39 | ▭ | ▭ | ▭ | ▭ |
| 20 | ▭ | ▭ | ▭ | ▭ | 40 | ▭ | ▭ | ▭ | ▭ |